Pearson Revise

T0351584

Pearson Edexcel GCSE (9–1)

Spanish

Second Edition

Revision Workbook

Series Consultant: Harry Smith

Author: Vivien Halksworth

Also available to support your revision:

Revise GCSE Study Skills Guide   9781292318875

The **Revise GCSE Study Skills Guide** is full of tried-and-trusted hints and tips for how to learn more effectively. It gives you techniques to help you achieve your best – throughout your GCSE studies and beyond!

Revise GCSE Revision Planner   9781292318868

The **Revise GCSE Revision Planner** helps you to plan and organise your time, step-by-step, throughout your GCSE revision. Use this book and wall chart to mastermind your revision.

Difficulty scale

The scale next to each exam-style question tells you how difficult it is.

Some questions cover a range of difficulties. The more of the scale that is shaded, the harder the question is.

 Some questions are Foundation level.

 Some questions are Higher level.

 Some questions are applicable to both levels.

For the full range of Pearson revision titles across KS2, 11+, KS3, GCSE, Functional Skills, AS/A Level and BTEC visit:
www.pearsonschools.co.uk/revise

Contents

1-to-1 page match with the Spanish Revision Guide ISBN 9781292412221

AUDIO

Audio files for the listening exercises in this book can be accessed by using the QR codes throughout the book, or going to www.pearsonschools.co.uk/mflrevisionaudio

Listen to the recording

A small bit of small print

Pearson Edexcel publishes Sample Assessment Material and the Specification on its website. This is the official content and this book should be used in conjunction with it. The questions in this Workbook have been written to help you practise every topic in the book. Remember: the real exam questions may not look like this.

Physical descriptions

My new friend

1 Read the text that Jaime received from his Peruvian friend Santi.

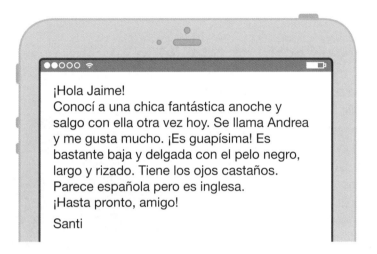

¡Hola Jaime!
Conocí a una chica fantástica anoche y salgo con ella otra vez hoy. Se llama Andrea y me gusta mucho. ¡Es guapísima! Es bastante baja y delgada con el pelo negro, largo y rizado. Tiene los ojos castaños. Parece española pero es inglesa.
¡Hasta pronto, amigo!

Santi

What is Andrea like?

Put a cross [×] in each one of the **three** correct boxes.

A	tall and slim	☐
B	small and slim	☐
C	long, black, curly hair	☐
D	short, black, curly hair	☐
E	grey eyes	☐
F	brown eyes	☐
G	Spanish	☐

(3 marks)

Changing your appearance

2 Some young people are talking about their appearance. Which aspect of it do they dislike?

Always listen to the recording twice before making your decision and writing your answer.

Listen to the recording and answer **in English**.

Guided

(a) …………………………… **(1 mark)**

Listen to the recording

(b) …………………………… **(1 mark)**

(c) …………………………… **(1 mark)**

(d) …………………………… **(1 mark)**

Character descriptions

A new TV series for children

1 Read this description of a new Spanish children's programme.

Una nueva serie de televisión

El martes empieza la nueva serie sobre las aventuras de cuatro chicos y su perro Tobi.

Lucas, el chico mayor, es atrevido y valiente pero siempre muy responsable. La chica mayor se llama Bea y es muy deportista, aunque a veces un poco egoísta, pero no hay nadie más leal a sus amigos.

Luego está Óscar, un chico más serio y muy inteligente. Puede ser tímido pero también es terco cuando sabe que tiene razón. La más joven es Alicia, una chica simpática y habladora, muy segura de sí misma a pesar de ser la menor.

Which adjective does **not describe each character**? Put a cross [×] in the correct box for each question.

(i) Lucas

☐	**A** brave
☐	**B** cheerful
☐	**C** daring
☐	**D** responsible

(ii) Bea

☐	**A** selfish
☐	**B** intelligent
☐	**C** loyal
☐	**D** sporty

(iii) Óscar

☐	**A** moody
☐	**B** serious
☐	**C** shy
☐	**D** stubborn

(iv) Alicia

☐	**A** chatty
☐	**B** likeable
☐	**C** self-confident
☐	**D** untidy

(4 marks)

Translation

2 Translate this passage **into Spanish.**

> When I was young I was a bit shy and very serious. Now I am more sure of myself and I am a reliable and optimistic person. My friends say that I am likeable and friendly.

I was = *era*
they say that = *dicen que*

Guided

....

....

....

....

(12 marks)

Describing family

Marta's family

1 Read this letter from Gemma's Spanish friend, Marta, about her family.

> ¡Hola Gemma!
> Antes de visitarnos en abril, deberías saber un poco de la familia con quien vas a vivir. Mis padres, Begoña y Pablo, están casados desde hace casi veinte años – es su aniversario pronto – han vivido en este pueblo toda la vida. Mi hermano, Diego, es el hijo mayor y se parece mucho a mi padre. De vez en cuando tienen alguna disputa pero nunca nada serio. Luego, estoy yo – dos años menor que Diego – y por fin, Lucía, la pequeña, que sólo tiene siete años. Nuestra abuela, Rosa, vive en la casa de al lado y comparte la casa con nuestro tío, Gabriel, que es divorciado. Estoy segura de que te va a gustar nuestra familia y nuestros parientes. ¡Son un poco ruidosos pero son muy amables!
> Un abrazo
> Marta

Complete the sentences by writing the correct name or names for each question. Enter either **Begoña**, **Diego**, **Lucía**, **Marta**, **Pablo**, **Rosa** or **Gabriel**. Some names may be used more than once or not at all.

> Be careful: **three** of the questions require two names.

A The couple married for 19 years are .... and ....

B The child who looks like one of their parents is ....

C The ones that argue occasionally are .... and ....

D The girl a bit younger than her brother is ....

E The youngest child is ....

F Their neighbours are .... and ....

G The uncle who is no longer married is ....   **(9 marks)**

Gemma's family

2 Gemma has recorded a description of her family for Marta.

Listen to the recording and complete the gap in each sentence using a word from the box below. There are more words than gaps.

Listen to the recording

> | badly | divorced | eight | room | sister | stepfather | stepbrother |
> | well | married | eleven | bed | brother | father | cousin |

Gemma's parents have been .... for .... years.

Gemma has one .... and they live with their mother and

.... When their .... visits for the weekend,

Gemma has to share a .... with her sister. They get on very

.... with David.   **(7 marks)**

Friends

Guided

Listen to the recording

The qualities of a friend

1   Your Spanish exchange partner's friends are talking about what is the **most** important quality of a friend.

Listen to the recording and put a cross [×] in the correct box for each question.

> The speakers mention more than one quality, so having to pick out the **one** quality that is the **most** important makes this a more challenging task.

(i)   Someone who …

☐	**A** shares your interests.
☐	**B** you can have fun with.
☐	**C** will always tell the truth.
☐	**D** has similar beliefs.

(ii)   Someone who …

☐	**A** shares your sense of humour.
☐	**B** is prepared to listen to you.
☐	**C** can see your point of view.
☐	**D** is of similar intelligence.

(iii)   Someone who …

☐	**A** will keep your secrets.
☐	**B** you have a good time with.
☐	**C** you can talk to.
☐	**D** boosts your self-confidence.

(iv)   Someone who …

☐	**A** is there for you.
☐	**B** helps with problems.
☐	**C** puts friendship before romance.
☐	**D** accepts you as you are.

(4 marks)

Guided

Listen to the recording

Los amigos

2   Mira la foto y prepara las respuestas a los siguientes puntos:

* la descripción de la foto

* el tipo de amigo/a que eres

* las cualidades del amigo/de la amiga ideal

* descripción de tu mejor amigo/a

* las actividades que haces con tus amigos/as

> Prepare your answers using the prompts. Then listen to the recording of the teacher's questions and answer in the pauses. There is a recording of one student's answers in the answer section to give you more ideas.

Role models

Celebrities as role models

1 Read this comment, posted by Eduardo on a Mexican website about celebrities.

> The options come in the same order as the text. It can be helpful to read the options first, before you tackle the text to find the answers.

● ● ●

Cuando era pequeño, siempre miraba a los famosos esperando ser como ellos un día. Intentaba imitarlos y pensaba que eran modelos responsables y maduros en todo lo que hacían. Ahora que soy un poco mayor, he cambiado de opinión y creo que, como todo el mundo, las personas famosas cometen errores y eso puede ser peligroso porque su comportamiento influye en los jóvenes.

Put a cross [×] in each one of the **three** correct boxes.

A	Eduardo felt differently about celebrities when he was a child.	☐
B	Eduardo thinks most celebrities are mature regarding their responsibilities.	☐
C	Celebrities do a lot to help charities.	☐
D	Eduardo now thinks that celebrities make mistakes.	☐
E	The example set by celebrities can even be dangerous.	☐
F	The fashion world has an unhealthy impact upon young people.	☐
G	Young people are sensible and don't react to the pressure.	☐

(3 marks)

Discussing celebrities

2 A guest on a Spanish TV chat show gives her views about celebrities.

Listen to the recording and put a cross [×] in each one of the **three** correct boxes.

Listen to the recording

A	Reporters often run stories on sports stars behaving badly.	☐
B	Fortunately there have been no cases of violence.	☐
C	They get away with possessing drugs because of who they are.	☐
D	Doping in sport is another bad example seen in the news.	☐
E	Celebrities must maintain standards of behaviour in public and in private.	☐
F	Cristina has seen celebrities working on behalf of fair trade.	☐
G	Some people think that celebrities do charity work for selfish reasons.	☐

(3 marks)

Relationships

Listen to the recording

A radio phone-in

1 You listen to a phone-in for advice about relationships. How does each person feel about the special person in their life?

Listen to the recording and complete the sentences. Choose between **enamorado/a**, **triste**, **confuso/a** and **enfadado/a**. You can use each word more than once.

(a) Sofía se siente .... **(1 mark)**

(b) Sebastián se siente .... **(1 mark)**

(c) Mariana se siente .... **(1 mark)**

(d) Alejandro se siente .... **(1 mark)**

(e) Gabriela se siente .... **(1 mark)**

Role play: una invitación

Guided

Listen to the recording

2 Your Spanish exchange partner, Miranda, is busy on Saturday but a friend of hers invites you both out for the day. The teacher will play the role of the friend and will speak first.

> Prepare your answers using the prompts. Then listen to the recording of the teacher's part and answer in the pauses. If you need more time, simply pause the recording. An example of a complete role play is recorded in the answer section.

You must address the friend as *tú*. You will talk to the teacher using the five prompts below.

Estás hablando con la amiga de tu amigo/a español/a. La amiga os invita a salir.

1 El problema de tu compañera

2 Tu aceptación y razón

3 Preferencia – playa o montaña – razón

4 **!**

5 **?** Relación con Miranda

> When accepting an invitation, you will need the conditional tense of *gustar*. To say 'Yes, I would really like that', you can say *'Sí, me gustaría mucho'* and then go on to give your reason.

When I was younger

> Guided

Entrevista con un escritor

1 You read an online interview with the author Carlos Vargas Márquez, who is describing his childhood.

Carlos, ¿cómo eras de niño?

De niño, pasaba bastante tiempo solo porque era hijo único pero tenía una gran imaginación. Si jugaba en mi dormitorio, imaginaba que la cama era una isla desierta en medio del mar. Cuando jugaba al aire libre, creía que el jardín era un bosque tropical con animales salvajes. No tenía mucho éxito como estudiante y no sacaba buenas notas, pero siempre leía mucho y escribía pequeñas historias.

Carlos Vargas Márquez

Answer the questions **in English.**

(a) Why did Carlos spend a lot of time alone? ....

.... **(1 mark)**

(b) In his imagination when he was playing, what did these things become?

   (i) his bed ....

   .... **(1 mark)**

   (ii) the garden ....

   .... **(1 mark)**

(c) What indicates that he did not find school engaging? ....

.... **(1 mark)**

(d) What were the early signs that he would become an author? ....

.... **(2 marks)**

> The number of marks is a clue to the amount of information expected in the answer. Make sure that you give **two** signs here.

Entrevista con un escritor

2 You listen to the second part of the interview online.

Listen to the recording and put a cross next to the **three** correct statements.

Listen to the recording

☐	**A**	He lived all his life in the country.
☐	**B**	He played outdoors a lot.
☐	**C**	His cousins bought him a bike.
☐	**D**	He played happily with his cousins.
☐	**E**	He looks back fondly on his childhood.

(3 marks)

Peer group pressure

A dreadful year

1   Read this story about a teenage girl's experience.

> Soy Natalia y siempre he sido una chica un poco atrevida pero el año pasado tomé unas decisiones muy poco inteligentes. Dejé de ver a mi mejor amiga, Sara, y empecé a salir con un grupo de chicos muy rebeldes. Pensé que eran emocionantes y animados, pero en realidad eran desagradables. Bajo su influencia comencé a ignorar a Sara e incluso a reírme de ella. Además, mis notas en el instituto empeoraron mucho. Un día, Sara vino a la casa y, convencida de que podría ayudarme, me mostró fotos de los días de antes cuando íbamos de compras juntas o salíamos al cine. Fue entonces cuando entendí la verdad sobre mis nuevos amigos y decidí abandonar ese grupo. ¡Y lo hice! Ahora soy una persona muy distinta, pero Sara es todavía mi mejor amiga.

Which adjectives describe each person or thing? Complete each sentence using a word from the box below. There are more words than gaps.

foolish	exciting	unpleasant	dishonest	negative	optimistic
adventurous	different	poor	positive	brave	sensible

(a) Natalia made decisions which were ....   **(1 mark)**

(b) Her new friends seemed ....   **(1 mark)**

(c) Her new friends were actually ....   **(1 mark)**

(d) Her friends' influences were ....   **(1 mark)**

(e) Natalia is now ....   **(1 mark)**

Un artículo sobre los amigos

2   Escribe un artículo para una revista sobre los amigos. **Debes** mencionar los puntos siguientes:

- describe a tu amigo/a
- sus problemas causados por la presión del grupo
- cómo tú lo/la ayudaste
- cómo están las cosas ahora.

Escribe aproximadamente 80–90 palabras **en español**.

....

....

....

....

....   **(20 marks)**

Customs

Spanish customs

Listen to the recording

1 Your Spanish friends are explaining some of their customs. What does each one say?

Listen to the recording and complete the sentences by putting a cross [×] in the correct box for each question.

(i) Having tapas is …

☐	**A** becoming popular outside Spain.
☐	**B** a snack rather than a full meal.
☐	**C** going out of fashion in Spain.
☐	**D** only possible in certain bars.

(iii) The bull fight …

☐	**A** is a very old custom.
☐	**B** attracts many protesters.
☐	**C** is still popular throughout Spain.
☐	**D** only uses bulls bred in the north.

(ii) The Spanish stroll …

☐	**A** is an after-lunch activity.
☐	**B** takes place in the main street.
☐	**C** always ends up with a cup of coffee.
☐	**D** doesn't happen on Sundays.

(iv) The siesta …

☐	**A** is taken throughout the year.
☐	**B** is needed because of the heat.
☐	**C** is becoming popular in Northern Europe.
☐	**D** is not possible for people who work.

(4 marks)

Customs

Guided

Listen to the recording

2 Mira la foto y prepara las respuestas a los siguientes puntos:

- la descripción de la foto
- una costumbre en tu casa
- la comida para una ocasión especial
- tu opinión sobre las costumbres españolas
- tu opinión sobre la idea de dormir la siesta en tu país

Describe esta foto.

Hay un grupo de personas al lado de una hoguera. Es el cinco de noviembre, una fiesta en Gran Bretaña. Hay fuegos artificiales y un ambiente alegre.

Prepare your answers using the prompts. Then listen to the recording of the teacher's questions and answer in the pauses. There is a recording of one student's answers in the answer section to give you more ideas.

Everyday life

A typical day for Rubén

Guided

1   You have asked your penfriend, Rubén, about his daily life and this is his reply.
    Read his email.

✉

Durante la semana me levanto a las siete menos cuarto, y cinco minutos después estoy en la ducha. Luego desayuno antes de que llegue el autobús a las siete y media. Voy al instituto con mis amigos y llegamos sobre las ocho menos diez.

Al final del día escolar, a las dos y media, volvemos a casa para comer. Mi madre prepara la comida y todos comemos sobre las tres. Después, descansamos un rato. Mis padres leen el periódico o ven la televisión y yo navego la red o chateo con amigos. Suelo empezar mis deberes sobre las cinco, después de que mi padre vuelva al trabajo, y estudio durante una hora o un poco más. Cuando termino, a veces voy a la casa de un amigo o juego al baloncesto en el parque.

Mi familia y yo normalmente cenamos a las nueve, mucho más tarde que mis amigos ingleses, y me acuesto a las once. Sin embargo, anoche no me dormí hasta la una porque vi una película en mi portátil. Mis padres estaban muy enfadados.

Answer the questions **in English**. You do not need to write in full sentences.

(a) What does Rubén do at 6.45? .... **(1 mark)**

(b) What do Rubén's parents do immediately after lunch? Mention **two** things.

.... **(2 marks)**

(c) What **two** things does Rubén often do after finishing his homework?

.... **(2 marks)**

(d) Why didn't Rubén get to sleep until late last night?

.... **(1 mark)**

(e) How did his parents react? .... **(1 mark)**

> The text gives two pieces of information in answer to question (d) (*película* + *portátil*) and both are relevant. It is sensible to include all relevant information in order to give the best possible answer.

Un fin de semana típico

2   Tu amigo mexicano quiere saber cómo pasas el fin de semana.

    Escríbele un correo electrónico. Menciona:

    • la hora cuando te levantas   • tus actividades normales

    • las comidas   • algo diferente que hiciste el fin de semana pasado.

    Escribe aproximadamente 40–50 palabras **en español**.

    ....

    ....

    ....

    ....

    .... **(16 marks)**

Meals at home

Cooking and eating

1   Some Spanish friends are talking about meals at home.

Listen to the recording and answer the questions **in English.**

(a) What does Carla say about her eating habits?

....   **(1 mark)**

(b) What is David telling his friends?

....   **(1 mark)**

(c) What does Nuria say about her family meals?

....   **(1 mark)**

(d) What change has Ricardo made to his diet?

....   **(1 mark)**

Meals at home

 Guided

2   Mira la foto y prepara las respuestas a los siguientes puntos:

•   la descripción de la foto

•   una comida típica en casa

•   las horas de las comidas en casa

•   lo que tomaste el fin de semana pasado

•   tu opinión sobre la comida en tu instituto

> Prepare your answers using the prompts. Then listen to the recording of the teacher's questions and answer in the pauses. There is a recording of one student's answers in the answer section to give you more ideas.

Food and drink

Listen to the recording

Eating out

1 You hear some young Spanish people talking about what they are going to eat or drink.

   Listen and complete the sentences with a word from the box. There are more words than gaps.

> flan   grapefruit   omelette   orange   pineapple
>
> sandwich   strawberry   toastie

(a) Magda is having a ham .... **(1 mark)**

(b) Pablo is having a .... yoghurt. **(1 mark)**

(c) María is having a cheese .... **(1 mark)**

(d) Santi is having .... juice. **(1 mark)**

Una cena de cumpleaños

2 Lee este email de tu amigo español, Jorge, que describe su cena de cumpleaños.

> ✉
>
> Anoche comimos en el mejor restaurante de mi pueblo para celebrar mi cumpleaños. A mí me gustaron más el atún y las sardinas. Mi padre prefirió las brochetas de pollo y el filete de cerdo.
> A mi hermano le gustó más el entrante de judías y guisantes. A mi hermana le gustó más el postre de melocotón y frambuesas. Mi madre pensó que lo mejor fueron los pinchos de cordero y las chuletas.

¿Qué aspecto de la cena le gustó más a cada miembro de la familia? Escoge entre **carne**, **pescado**, **verduras** o **fruta**. Puedes usar palabras más de una vez.

(a) Jorge prefirió .... **(1 mark)**   (d) Su hermana prefirió .... **(1 mark)**

(b) Su padre prefirió .... **(1 mark)**   (e) Su madre prefirió .... **(1 mark)**

(c) Su hermano prefirió .... **(1 mark)**

Guided

Translation

3 Translate this passage **into English.**

> Me gusta mucho ir de tapas porque puedes probar una variedad de platos.
> En Galicia, donde vivo, la especialidad es el pescado y anoche tomé mariscos en una salsa muy sabrosa.

I really like going ....

....

....

....

.... **(12 marks)**

Shopping for clothes

Shopping trends

1 Read what these people say about shopping. Where does each person prefer to shop? Enter either Elvira, Antonia or Pepito. Some names may be used more than once or not at all.

Elvira

No entiendo por qué a la gente le gusta ir de compras. El supermercado está bastante lejos de mi casa y siempre está lleno de gente. Por eso nunca voy allí, y hago la compra en la tienda que está al lado de mi casa porque es más práctico.

Antonia

Yo no soy aficionada a comprar. Sin embargo, me gusta estar a la moda. Últimamente muchos de mis amigos hacen fiestas para vender ropa y maquillaje, y eso me gusta. ¡Ganan dinero también!

Pepito

Normalmente compro en las tiendas de uno de los centros comerciales que hay en Burgos. Me encanta la variedad y suelen ser más baratos. ¡Es la mejor manera de comprar! De vez en cuando también compro por Internet.

A supermarkets ....

B sales parties ....

C local shops ....

D the market ....

E shopping centres ....

F mail order ....

(3 marks)

Shopping preferences

2 (a) Why doesn't Ana like the shops in her neighbourhood?

.... **(1 mark)**

(b) What **two** things does Inés do instead of buying things?

.... **(2 marks)**

(c) How does Ricardo prefer to shop? .... **(1 mark)**

Role play: shopping

3 While on an exchange visit to Spain, your exchange partner, Camila, asks what you would like to do. The teacher will play the role of Camila and will speak first.

You must address Camila as *tú*. You will talk to the teacher using the five prompts below.

> Prepare your answers using the prompts. Then listen to the recording of the teacher's part and answer in the pauses. If you need more time, simply pause the recording. An example of a complete role play is recorded in the answer section.

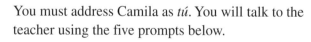

Estás con tu amiga española y te pregunta qué quieres hacer.

1 Ir de compras – tu razón

2 Dónde y tu razón

3 Cosas para comprar

4 !

5 ? Opinión sobre ir de compras

Social media

Opinions on social media

Laura	Acabo de cerrar mi cuenta porque me molestaba leer la misma basura todo el tiempo. No quería ver más vídeos de mascotas haciendo cosas divertidas ni las fotos de las vacaciones de todo el mundo. Francamente, me aburrió.
Jaime	Yo creo que a veces la gente es demasiado honesta con lo que dice en esas páginas. Imagina que vas a una entrevista y, después, el empresario mira tu página en una red social. ¿Hay información allí que no quieres que vea? Pues cuidado.
Mariana	Soy profesora y me ha sorprendido que estas redes también puedan usarse en la enseñanza. Resulta que una de mis clases ha creado una página y los estudiantes pueden escribir preguntas allí que sus compañeros contestan. ¡Qué maravilla!
Teo	Para mí, estas páginas son muy divertidas pero una distracción terrible. Cuando estoy haciendo mis deberes en el ordenador, siempre estoy contestando los mensajes que aparecen en la pantalla en lugar de concentrarme en escribir mi ensayo.

1   Who says what about social networks?

Enter either **Laura**, **Jaime**, **Mariana** or **Teo** in the gaps below. Some names may be used twice or not at all.

(a) .... warns people to beware of what they write.   **(1 mark)**

(b) .... has just closed a social media account.   **(1 mark)**

(c) .... finds that social networks stop you doing what you should be doing.   **(1 mark)**

(d) .... is impressed by the way some young people use social networks.   **(1 mark)**

(e) .... is concerned that a company boss might look at an applicant's page.   **(1 mark)**

(f) .... would recommend them as a useful educational tool.   **(1 mark)**

Las redes sociales

2   Decides contribuir a un blog sobre el uso de las redes sociales.

Escribe tus ideas para el blog.

> **Guided**

Debes mencionar los puntos siguientes:

- lo que te gusta de las redes sociales
- lo que te preocupa de las redes sociales
- cómo has usado una red social recientemente
- cómo vas a usar las redes sociales este fin de semana y por qué.

Escribe aproximadamente 80–90 palabras **en español**. Escribe la respuesta en una hoja de papel.

Me gusta usar las redes sociales para ver lo que hacen mis amigos y

....

....

....   **(20 marks)**

Technology

Listen to the recording

Opinions of technology

1   Your Spanish friend Sara is talking to you about technology.

Listen and complete the sentences using the words from the box. There are more words than gaps.

| broken | old | laptop | mouse | screen |
| slow | tablet | well designed | | |

Sara's computer is really .... She thinks the keyboard

is ....

She doesn't want a .... because she prefers a computer

with a separate ....

(4 marks)

Listen to the recording

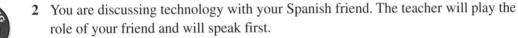

Role play: technology

2   You are discussing technology with your Spanish friend. The teacher will play the role of your friend and will speak first.

You must address the friend as *tú*. You will talk to the teacher using the five prompts below.

> Prepare your answers using the prompts. Then listen to the recording of the teacher's part and answer in the pauses. If you need more time, simply pause the recording. An example of a complete role play is recorded in the answer section.

Estás hablando de tecnología con tu amigo español / tu amiga española.

1   Tu uso de la tecnología

2   Tu opinión de las tabletas

3   **!**

4   El coste de la tecnología

5   **?** Página web favorita

> For the unprepared point, it is of course essential to listen carefully to the question you are being asked. However, it is fine to ask your teacher to repeat the question, twice at the most.
> To do so, you can say: *¿Puedes repetirlo?* (Can you repeat it?) or *Más despacio, por favor* (More slowly, please).

The internet

Internet for all ages

1 Read Jorge's account of how his family uses the internet.

Who uses the internet in these ways? Enter either **Jorge**, **padre**, **Cristina** or **madre**. You can use each person more than once.

> En mi casa somos muy aficionados a Internet y sus muchos usos. Yo soy Jorge y soy estudiante en la universidad. Uso Internet para buscar información y hacer investigaciones. También suelo bajar canciones, usar las redes sociales y subir fotos. Mi padre siempre está mandando y recibiendo correos electrónicos relacionados con su trabajo. Incluso mi hermana pequeña, Cristina, usa Internet para jugar a juegos educativos o ver vídeos para niños. Mi madre estudia inglés y le gusta hacer los ejercicios interactivos para practicar.

(a) .... does online exercises to learn a language.   **(1 mark)**

(b) .... plays games.   **(1 mark)**

(c) .... uses email constantly.   **(1 mark)**

(d) .... downloads music.   **(1 mark)**

(e) .... watches videos.   **(1 mark)**

Using the internet

2 Some Spanish friends are discussing their use of the internet. How do they use it?

Listen to the recording and put a cross [×] in each one of the **three** correct boxes.

Listen to the recording

A	sending messages	☐
B	looking for work	☐
C	playing games	☐
D	social networking	☐
E	online shopping	☐
F	booking flights	☐
G	surfing the web	☐

(3 marks)

Translation

3 Translate this passage **into English**. Write your answer on a separate piece of paper.

Guided

> Yo no puedo imaginar la vida sin Internet porque en mi casa solemos usarlo todos los días. Si olvidas el nombre de una película o quieres saber cuándo nació cierto autor, Internet tiene todas las repuestas. Además, la manera en que hacemos nuestras compras ahora es diferente.

I can't imagine life without the internet ....

....   **(12 marks)**

Pros and cons of technology

Concerns about technology

Listen to the recording

1 Four Spanish friends are discussing their concerns about technology. Listen to the recording and complete the sentences by putting a cross [×] in the correct box for each question.

(i) Pedro has just had a lesson in …

☐	**A** maths
☐	**B** IT
☐	**C** science
☐	**D** food technology

(ii) Luisa knows a girl who …

☐	**A** had her identity stolen.
☐	**B** sent money to a swindler.
☐	**C** was upset by online bullying.
☐	**D** bought tickets that never arrived.

(iii) Rafael's father …

☐	**A** refuses to make any purchases online.
☐	**B** had his bank account hacked from abroad.
☐	**C** went into the bank when he suspected fraud.
☐	**D** has set up security controls on his account.

(iv) Sandra …

☐	**A** hopes to meet someone on a dating site.
☐	**B** showed her parents how to set controls.
☐	**C** met someone she got to know online.
☐	**D** worries about what sites young children might see.

(v) Pedro …

☐	**A** says that technology is making us lazy.
☐	**B** has problems with his internet connection.
☐	**C** thinks that mobiles make us ignore each other.
☐	**D** forgot a tennis match because he was online.

(5 marks)

Lo bueno y lo malo de Internet

Listen to the recording

Prepare your answers using the prompts. Then listen to the recording of the teacher's questions and answer in the pauses. There is a recording of one student's answers in the answer section to give you more ideas.

2 Mira la foto y prepara las respuestas a los siguientes puntos:

- la descripción de la foto
- tu opinión sobre los problemas de Internet
- tu opinión sobre los aspectos buenos de Internet
- lo que hiciste en Internet anoche
- !

Hobbies

Favourite hobbies

1 Read these contributions to a forum about birthday presents.

Adela	Lo ideal para mí sería ropa de deporte de mi marca favorita. No me interesan ni los libros ni la música.
Benjamín	Lo que yo quiero es aprender a tocar la batería: cinco clases gratuitas serían perfectas. Nada de equipo de deporte.
Sara	El año pasado recibí un vídeo de dibujos animados de mi tía. ¡Qué infantil! Este año me gustarían dos entradas para el torneo de baloncesto.
Nicolás	Lo peor es cuando recibes calcetines o camisetas. Me aburre un montón. El mejor regalo: un nuevo móvil – el último modelo.

Who says what about birthday presents? Enter either **Adela**, **Benjamín**, **Sara** or **Nicolás**. You can use each person more than once.

(a) ……………………………………… would like sportswear.   **(1 mark)**

(b) ……………………………………… does not want to be given clothes.   **(1 mark)**

(c) ……………………………………… wants to watch a live match.   **(1 mark)**

(d) ……………………………………… wants music tuition.   **(1 mark)**

Mis pasatiempos

2 Quieres ir a España para trabajar en un club de niños en un camping.

Escribe un email al jefe.

Menciona:

- los deportes que haces
- los otros pasatiempos que tienes
- cuándo haces estas actividades
- por qué te gustan las actividades.

Escribe unas 40–50 palabras **en español**.

………………………………………………………………………………

………………………………………………………………………………

………………………………………………………………………………

………………………………………………………………………………

………………………………………………………………………………

………………………………………………………………………………

………………………………………………………………………………

> Remember: when talking about playing an instrument, use the verb *tocar* for 'to play'. However, for 'playing' a game or sport you use *jugar*. When talking about 'doing' an activity, such as riding or skating, you use *hacer*.

(16 marks)

Music

A music blog

1 Read the blog entries from a discussion about music.

> **Blog de música. Escribe tu opinión o tus experiencias.**
>
> **David:** Mi padre nunca tuvo la oportunidad de aprender un instrumento cuando era joven así que mañana empieza clases de guitarra. Yo uso la música para ayudarme a hacer los trabajos que no me gustan. No me importa lavar el coche o arreglar mi dormitorio si puedo escuchar música.
>
> **Eduardo:** Mi grupo favorito dio un concierto anoche pero fue una pena que sólo cantaran las canciones de su nuevo álbum. Fue un poco decepcionante. Canto con un coro una vez a la semana y es muy relajante. Pero ahora estoy nervioso porque damos un concierto este viernes.
>
> **Fernando:** A veces no quería ir a las clases de piano cuando era pequeño, pero ahora, tocar el piano es lo que más me gusta en la vida. Practiqué con la banda ayer y a todos les gustan las canciones que he escrito. ¡Genial!

Who says the following? Enter either **David**, **Eduardo** or **Fernando**. You can use each person more than once.

(a) .... is glad he carried on with his music lessons.   **(1 mark)**

(b) .... says that the idea of performing is a bit nerve-racking.   **(1 mark)**

(c) .... felt that it was a shame the band didn't play their old hits.   **(1 mark)**

(d) .... is relieved that the group likes his songs.   **(1 mark)**

(e) .... thinks that music is useful to take your mind off boring jobs.   **(1 mark)**

Juan Zelada, musician

2 This person is talking about an interview he has had with Juan Zelada.

Listen to the recording and answer the questions below **in English.**

Listen to the recording

(a) Why does Juan say he is here? ....   **(1 mark)**

(b) What does he say about

    (i) breakfast? ....   **(1 mark)**

    (ii) his music? ....   **(1 mark)**

(c) What does he usually do

    (i) in the mornings? ....   **(1 mark)**

    (ii) in the evenings? ....   **(1 mark)**

(d) Why does he say he doesn't sleep? ....   **(1 mark)**

(e) What does he do once every week? ....   **(1 mark)**

(f) Why does he do this? ....   **(1 mark)**

Sport

Beach volleyball

1 Read this advert. Complete the sentences by putting a cross [×] in the correct box.

Gran Fiesta Voleibol Playa

¿No sabes qué hacer estas vacaciones?
¿Quieres hacer ejercicio pero también buscas mucha diversión?
¡Pues esta fiesta es para ti!
Para jóvenes de entre trece y diecisiete años, este curso es ideal no sólo para mejorar tus habilidades deportivas – especialmente las de equipo – sino que también es una gran oportunidad para conocer nuevos amigos.
Si te interesa …
Ven el día lunes 3 a la cala de Mogán – zona verde.
Trae bañador, ropa deportiva y comida
(todos los refrescos están incluidos).
Precio: 15 euros el día.
Imprescindible autorización de padres o tutores.
Nuestras instalaciones son aptas para gente con discapacidades.

(i) This activity is for people who want to have …

☐	A	a rest.
☐	B	fun.
☐	C	a holiday.
☐	D	a summer job.

(ii) The festival is for …

☐	A	all ages.
☐	B	parents.
☐	C	young children.
☐	D	teenagers.

(iii) One skill you might improve is …

☐	A	speaking another language.
☐	B	time management.
☐	C	communication.
☐	D	being a team player.

(iv) You need to bring …

☐	A	a ball.
☐	B	drinks.
☐	C	appropriate clothing.
☐	D	friends.

(v) Participation will not be possible without …

☐	A	parental consent.
☐	B	a sporting qualification.
☐	C	pre-booking.
☐	D	some form of identification.

(5 marks)

Sport

2 You overhear three young people talking about sport. Which sports do they mention?

Listen to the recording and put a cross [×] in each one of the **three** correct boxes.

Listen to the recording

A	cycling	☐
B	swimming	☐
C	athletics	☐
D	basketball	☐
E	skiing	☐
F	skating	☐
G	horse riding	☐

> For this type of question, use the five-minute reading time at the start of the exam to read the sports and think about what they are in Spanish. That way you will be better prepared to listen out for the ones that come up.

(3 marks)

Reading

LISTENING TRACK 23

Opinions about reading

1 Your Spanish friend, Daniela, is talking about her sister and brothers.
What do they like to read?

Listen to the recording and put a cross [×] in each one of the **three** correct boxes.

Listen to the recording

A	classical novels	☐
B	digital newspapers	☐
C	e-books	☐
D	modern fiction	☐
E	crime stories	☐
F	biographies	☐
G	magazines	☐

(3 marks)

Your opinions on reading

SPEAKING TRACK 24

> Guided

Listen to the recording

> Prepare your answers using the prompts. Then listen to the recording of the teacher's questions and answer in the pauses. There is a recording of one student's answers in the answer section to give you more ideas.

2 Mira la foto y prepara las respuestas a los siguientes puntos:

- la descripción de la foto
- tu opinión sobre leer
- un beneficio de la lectura
- tu opinión de los libros electrónicos
- lo que hiciste ayer para relajarte

> When you are asked to give opinions, you can use verbs such as *me gusta(n)* and *me encanta(n)* or adjectives such as *útil, práctico, informativo*.

Films

Film descriptions

1 What type of films are showing at the cinema?

Listen to the recording and put a cross [×] in each one of the **three** correct boxes.

Listen to the recording

A	an adventure film	☐
B	a cartoon	☐
C	a science-fiction film	☐
D	a sporting success story	☐
E	a horror film	☐
F	a historical drama	☐
G	a crime thriller	☐

(3 marks)

Sara y las goleadoras **by Laura Gallego**

2 Read the extract from the text. The girls are members of a football team arranging to go out.

—Oye, yo voy a ir este sábado al cine con unas amigas, ¿por qué no os venís Vicky y tú, y las que queráis? —dijo Lidia.

—Vicky no querrá, tiene que estudiar; y a Eva seguro que sus padres no la dejan —Sara contestó—. Pero lo diré a las demás; seguro que alguna se apunta. ¡Qué buena idea!

Ángela y Alicia tenían ganas de ir, e Isa y Julia también estuvieron de acuerdo, de modo que terminaron siendo un grupo muy numeroso.

Lo pasaron bien en el cine, y después fueron a merendar, y se rieron mucho comentando los mejores momentos de la película (Isa hizo una magistral imitación, muy dramática, de la actriz protagonista).

Answer the questions **in English**.

(a) Why won't Vicky go?.. **(1 mark)**

(b) Why does Sara think Eva won't go?................................. **(1 mark)**

(c) How do we know they had fun? Give **one** reason.................... **(1 mark)**

(d) What did they discuss afterwards?................................ **(1 mark)**

(e) How did Isa entertain them?..................................... **(1 mark)**

TV

TV programmes

1 Read José's list of favourite TV programmes. What is on his list? Put a cross [×] in the **four** correct boxes.

A	sports programmes	☐
B	cartoons	☐
C	quiz shows	☐
D	documentaries	☐
E	news	☐
F	music concerts	☐
G	soaps	☐

las noticias

los dibujos animados

las telenovelas

los documentales

las películas de terror

(4 marks)

Marisa's viewing habits

2 Marisa is talking about television programmes. Listen to the recording and complete the sentences. Use the correct words from the box. There are more words than gaps.

> sports programmes   soaps   adventure programmes   boring   interesting
>
> films   documentaries   rubbish   reality TV   cartoons

Listen to the recording

(a) Best of all she likes watching .... **(1 mark)**

(b) She can't stand .... **(1 mark)**

(c) She never watches .... **(1 mark)**

(d) She says soaps are .... **(1 mark)**

La televisión

3 Tu amiga Marta te pregunta sobre lo que ves en la televisión.

Escribe una respuesta.

Debes mencionar los puntos siguientes:

- cuándo te gusta ver la televisión
- tus programas favoritos
- los programas que no te gustan
- los programas que ves con tu familia.

Escribe aproximadamente 80–90 palabras **en español**. Escribe la respuesta en una hoja de papel.

....

....

....

.... **(20 marks)**

Celebrations

Special days

1 Read these accounts of celebrations on a forum.

Beatriz	La Nochevieja siempre es muy divertida en mi casa y el año pasado mis padres dieron una fiesta. A medianoche, claro, celebramos con las doce uvas, intentando comer una uva cada vez que sonaba* la campana.**
Emilio	En mi casa mantenemos la vieja costumbre de dar regalos de navidad el día de Reyes. Solo podemos abrir un regalo el día de Navidad, y tenemos que esperar hasta el seis de enero para abrir los demás.
Paula	De niña, me gustaba la Nochebuena porque había una cena especial y siempre empezábamos con marisco. Era una tarde emocionante porque toda la familia se reunía para celebrar la ocasión.
Santi	En Inglaterra, las fiestas navideñas son un poco diferentes. Siempre abren los regalos la mañana del 25 de diciembre y comen la comida principal sobre la una o las dos. ¡Muchas personas se duermen después!

sonar = to chime   **la campana* = bell

Answer the questions by entering either **Beatriz**, **Emilio**, **Paula** or **Santi**. You can use each person more than once.

(a) Who talks about Christmas Eve? ………………………………… **(1 mark)**

(b) Who talks about 6 January? ………………………………… **(1 mark)**

(c) Who mentions eating fruit? ………………………………… **(1 mark)**

(d) Who mentions eating seafood? ………………………………… **(1 mark)**

(e) Who talks about Christmas lunch? ………………………………… **(1 mark)**

(f) Who celebrates in a traditional way? ………………………………… **(1 mark)**

Special events

2 You hear a trailer about today's soap opera episodes. What celebrations are taking place?

Listen to the recording and put a cross [×] in each one of the **three** correct boxes.

> **Guided**

Listen to the recording

> Always listen to the whole recording and try not to base your answer on just hearing one word. For example, if you hear *matrimonio* you will need to keep listening so that you can decide whether it is a wedding or a wedding anniversary.

A	birth of baby	☐
B	New Year	☐
C	anniversary	☐
D	wedding	☐
E	retirement	☐
F	saint's day	☐
G	birthday	☐

(3 marks)

Festivals

A religious festival

1 Read the description of a Spanish religious festival.

> En muchos pueblos de la costa, la Virgen del Carmen tiene un significado especial porque es la santa patrona de los pescadores y los marineros. Además, en Málaga, se dice que la Virgen también se encarga de cuidar a todos los que se asocian con el mar, hasta a los que nadan o hacen windsurf. El dieciséis de julio, la gente del pueblo lleva la estatua de la Virgen al puerto. Entonces la ponen en un barco decorado con luces y flores. Luego la Virgen da una vuelta por la bahía* en el barco, acompañada de música y una procesión de otros barcos.

bahía = bay

Answer the questions **in English**.

(a) What else do the people of Málaga believe about the *Virgen del Carmen*?

....

.... **(1 mark)**

(b) Where do the villagers first take the statue of the Virgin?

.... **(1 mark)**

(c) Where is the statue then placed? Give full details.

.... **(1 mark)**

(d) Where is the figure then taken?

.... **(1 mark)**

(e) What accompaniment is provided?

.... **(1 mark)**

> Look for key vocabulary in the questions that will guide you to the answer in the text. In question (e), the word 'accompaniment' should direct you to *acompañada* in the text.

A historical festival

2 Cristina is talking about a festival in her home town, Alcoy: 'Los Moros* y Cristianos'.

Listen to the recording and put a cross [×] in each one of the **three** correct boxes.

Listen to the recording

A	There is a re-enactment of a historic battle.	☐
B	The festival commemorates a battle from 80 years ago.	☐
C	The Moors seize the castle from the Christians.	☐
D	The locals are happy to cover the cost of the festival.	☐
E	The festival attracts people from home and abroad.	☐
F	The noise can be excessive at times.	☐
G	People are considerate and don't leave litter behind.	☐

*los Moros – the Moors, people from North Africa

(3 marks)

Holiday preferences

Preferencias para las vacaciones

1   Lee el texto sobre las preferencias para las vacaciones.

> **Juan:** Yo creo que irse de vacaciones es una idea estupenda, pero preferiría ir después de los exámenes del colegio. Como ya tengo dieciséis años, preferiría pasar las vacaciones con mis amigos en vez de con mis padres, como de costumbre. Así que a partir del diez de junio me vendría bien, porque mi amigo Carlos tiene el último examen el día anterior. Es bastante difícil decidir adónde ir porque somos seis. Todos quieren ir a Grecia, pero yo no estoy tan seguro. Creo que hará demasiado calor.
>
> **María:** No me interesa para nada irme de vacaciones con mis amigos. Dentro de tres meses cumplo dieciocho años, pero no tengo ganas de estar lejos de mi familia, como muchos jóvenes. De hecho, pienso pasar mis vacaciones este año con mis hermanas. La semana que viene vamos a ir juntas a una agencia de viajes para organizar un viaje de tres semanas a México. Es el momento ideal, ya que de momento, mi tío está trabajando allí. Si no aprovechamos esta oportunidad, será una pena, porque en casa de mi tío no tenemos que pagar alojamiento.

Pon una cruz [×] en las **tres** casillas correctas.

A	Juan y María quieren viajar con sus amigos.	☐
B	Juan todavía no ha decidido adónde ir.	☐
C	A Juan le gusta pasar las vacaciones al sol.	☐
D	A María le preocupa lo que va a costar.	☐
E	Juan y María van a celebrar su cumpleaños.	☐
F	María va a reservar sus vacaciones la semana que viene.	☐
G	Juan y María están preocupados por los exámenes.	☐

(3 marks)

Holiday plans

2   You hear two Spanish friends, Chus and Enrique, talking about their holiday plans.

Listen to the recording and complete the sentences by putting a cross [×] in the correct box for each question.

Guided

Listen to the recording

(i)   What holiday is Chus recommending?

☐	A	six days in Andalusia
☐	B	a week in Austria
☐	C	a week on the coast
☐	D	ten days by the sea

(iii) What does Chus recommend about Ibiza?

☐	A	the sensational water sports
☐	B	spending time in the capital
☐	C	the night life
☐	D	sun, sea and sand

(ii) Why does Enrique prefer Cantabria?

☐	A	It's cheaper.
☐	B	It's easier by car.
☐	C	It's a shorter journey.
☐	D	The food is nicer there.

(iv) What happens in the end?

☐	A	Chus persuades Enrique to go for her idea.
☐	B	Chus accepts Enrique's plan.
☐	C	Chus decides to go on holiday without Enrique.
☐	D	Chus says that Enrique always gets his way.

(4 marks)

Hotels

Reservations

1 Read these extracts from hotel bookings.

Nos gustaría reservar un apartamento en la planta baja. Tengo movilidad reducida y tengo problemas para subir las escaleras.
Andrea

Preferimos una habitación en la parte de detrás del hotel, de las que dan al mar, porque en el otro lado, las vistas de las montañas no son tan bonitas.
Carlos

Si es posible, queremos una habitación lejos del ascensor porque, según nuestra experiencia, puede ser bastante ruidoso allí con la gente subiendo y bajando.
Begoña

Por lo que nos dicen los amigos, no basta con dejar abiertas las ventanas durante la noche. Para dormir hace falta el aire acondicionado.
David

What has each guest specifically mentioned? Enter either **Andrea**, **Begoña**, **Carlos** or **David**.
Some names may be used more than once.

(a) ………………………………… prefers to be away from the lift. **(1 mark)**

(b) ………………………………… has requested to be on the ground floor. **(1 mark)**

(c) ………………………………… is concerned about keeping cool. **(1 mark)**

(d) ………………………………… does not want to be at the front of the building. **(1 mark)**

Mr Gómez books a hotel

2 Listen to Mr Gómez making a reservation. Answer the questions below **in English**.

(a) What are **two** benefits of taking the family room instead of two rooms?

▷ **Guided**

Listen to the recording

………………………………………………………………………………………………… **(2 marks)**

(b) Which facilities are available in the room? Put a cross [×] in each one of the **three** correct boxes.

A	internet connection	☐
B	coffee-making facilities	☐
C	fridge	☐
D	phone	☐
E	shower	☐
F	air conditioning	☐
G	balcony	☐

(3 marks)

(c) How many nights will they be staying? ……………………………… **(1 mark)**

Camping

A camping holiday

1 Lucas leaves a voicemail message for Alejandro about their planned camping holiday.

Listen to the recording and put a cross [×] in the correct box for each question.

Listen to the
recording

(i) What does Lucas say about the camping equipment?

☐	**A**	The campsite will have everything they need.
☐	**B**	They can hire any necessary equipment once they are there.
☐	**C**	They will need to take everything they need with them.
☐	**D**	They are going to have to buy quite a lot of equipment.

(ii) What does Lucas say about the tent?

☐	**A**	They will probably need to buy a two-man tent.
☐	**B**	Lucas has a couple of one-man tents.
☐	**C**	Two people could fit easily into his tent.
☐	**D**	He is glad Alejandro has a good-sized tent.

(iii) What does Lucas say about the campsite facilities?

☐	**A**	There are washing facilities.
☐	**B**	There is a food shop.
☐	**C**	There is a games room.
☐	**D**	There is a café.

(iv) What does Lucas say about the location of the campsite?

☐	**A**	It's on the coast.
☐	**B**	It's by a river.
☐	**C**	It's near a mountain lake.
☐	**D**	It's on the outskirts of town.

(4 marks)

Role play: booking a campsite

> Prepare your answers using the prompts. Then listen to the recording of the teacher's part and answer in the pauses. If you need more time, simply pause the recording. An example of a complete role play is recorded in the answer section.

Guided

Listen to the
recording

2 You are phoning a Spanish campsite and want to reserve a pitch *(una parcela)*. The teacher will play the part of the booking clerk and will speak first.

You must address the booking clerk as *usted*. You will talk to the teacher using the five prompts below.

> When using the formal 'you' *(usted)*, you use the third person singular of the verb. For example: *¿Tiene usted …?* Do you have …?

Usted está hablando por teléfono con el empleado/la empleada del camping y quiere reservar una parcela.

1 Reserva – número de personas y tiendas

2 Número de noches y fecha de llegada

3 **!**

4 Una cosa que necesitas alquilar

5 **?** Instalaciones en el camping

Accommodation

Opinions about accommodation

1 Read these opinions. What do they like or dislike?

Pili	Me encantan los hoteles. Me gusta no tener que hacer mi cama ni ayudar en nada. Allí hay gente que te lo hace todo. ¡Es genial!
Pablo	Me gustan las actividades al aire libre. Soy una persona sencilla y no necesito muchos lujos.
Maruja	Lo que a mí me gusta es poder practicar mis deportes preferidos, tengo un kayak y me gusta nadar largas distancias. Es muy difícil hacerlo en la ciudad donde vivo.
Juli	No soy aficionado a las vacaciones en hoteles. Prefiero pasar mis vacaciones en casa de la familia o los amigos.

Enter either **Pili**, **Pablo**, **Maruja** or **Juli** in the gaps below. Some names may be used twice or not at all.

> Watch out for negative expressions such as *no … ni.*

(a) .... likes watersports.

(b) .... doesn't like to be indoors.

(c) .... doesn't like work.

(d) .... cares more about whom to spend a holiday with.   **(4 marks)**

Where to go

2 Your Spanish friends are talking about where they go on holiday.

Listen to their conversation and answer the following questions **in English**.

> Always look at the example to see how much information is required. Here, you need to give the accommodation **and** the location.

Listen to the recording

(a) Where does Paulina always go? ....   **(1 mark)**

(b) Where does Rogelio love to go? ....   **(1 mark)**

(c) Where does Samuel go with his friends? ....   **(1 mark)**

(d) Where does Eva's family always go? ....   **(1 mark)**

Holiday destinations

The ideal holiday

1 Read what these young people say about their ideal holidays.

Renata	Me interesa la vida nocturna de verano en mi ciudad y los centros comerciales, los museos y las galerías. Me gusta el ruido y la actividad. Odiaría una estancia en el campo.
Rahesh	Ya que mi estación del año favorito es el invierno, iré a un país famoso por la nieve y deportes como el alpinismo y el esquí. La idea de descansar en la playa no me apetece.
Luisa	Iré a países lejanos y distintos para ver la cultura, experimentar costumbres nuevas y probar platos picantes. Lo peor para mí serían unas vacaciones deportivas.
Li Jun	Una ciudad llena de discotecas y bares no me atrae. Siempre escogeré la tranquilidad de los espacios verdes para andar o ir en bicicleta y escapar del estrés de la vida urbana.

Who says what about their ideal holiday?

Enter either **Renata**, **Rahesh**, **Luisa** or **Li Jun** in the gaps below. Some names may be used twice or not at all.

(a) …………………………………… hopes to travel to faraway places.   **(1 mark)**

(b) …………………………………… would not like to go away in summer.   **(1 mark)**

(c) …………………………………… would choose a holiday in the countryside.   **(1 mark)**

(d) …………………………………… is keen to try foreign food.   **(1 mark)**

> It is not a good idea to base your answer on one word that you have read. It is essential to take the whole of the texts into account. For example, Renata mentions *una estancia en el campo* but, in fact, this is something she would hate.

Holiday destinations

2 Your Spanish friends have told you about their holiday preferences.

Listen to the recording and complete the sentences **in English**.

Listen to the recording

(a) Carlos wants to go to the …………………………………………………   **(1 mark)**

(b) Elena prefers to go to the …………………………………………………   **(1 mark)**

(c) Juan likes going to the …………………………………………………   **(1 mark)**

(d) Cristina wants to spend time in the …………………………………………   **(1 mark)**

(e) Pedro prefers to go to a …………………………………………………   **(1 mark)**

Travelling

Travel arrangements

1   Read the texts about travel arrangements.

●●○○○ 🛜   🔋▮

PRIYA

Llegaré a la estación a las tres. Es el autocar número 6.

●●○○○ 🛜   🔋▮

JOÃO

Papá, he perdido el último tren. ¿Podrías venir a buscarme?

●●○○○ 🛜   🔋▮

CARMEN

Pedro, si compras un billete para Medellín, ¿me compras uno también?

●●○○○ 🛜   🔋▮

DAVID

El tren debería salir en dos minutos pero hay un retraso.

●●○○○ 🛜   🔋▮

ELAF

No hay un tren directo. Vamos a tener que cambiar dos veces.

●●○○○ 🛜   🔋▮

FRANCISCO

¿Cuánto tiempo dura el viaje? No queremos llegar de noche.

Answer the following questions **in English**. You do not need to write in full sentences.

(a)   What does João need his dad to do? ………………………………………   **(1 mark)**

(b)   What does Carmen ask Pedro to do? ………………………………………   **(1 mark)**

(c)   What is David's problem? ………………………………………………   **(1 mark)**

(d)   What will Elaf have to do on her journey? ………………………………   **(1 mark)**

(e)   When does Francisco want to arrive? ………………………………………   **(1 mark)**

Role play: arranging to visit a friend

Prepare your answers using the prompts. Then listen to the recording of the teacher's part and answer in the pauses. If you need more time, simply pause the recording. An example of a complete role play is recorded in the answer section.

Listen to the recording

2   You are phoning your Spanish friend to confirm the details of your stay with him/her. The teacher will play the part of your friend and will speak first.

You must address your friend as *tú*. You will talk to the teacher using the five prompts below.

Llamas a tu amigo/a para confirmar los detalles de tu visita a su casa.

1   Día y hora de tu llegada

2   Tu viaje – transporte y sitio de llegada

3   **!**

4   **?** Tu llegada a la casa – cómo

5   **?** El coste de un taxi a la casa

> You will find this vocabulary useful:
> luggage – *el equipaje*; suitcase – *la maleta*;
> bag – *la bolsa*; rucksack – *la mochila*.

Holiday activities

On holiday

1 Read what these people say about holidays on a website forum.

Who says what about holiday activities? Enter either **Tanvi**, **Ali**, **Mario** or **Daniela**. You can use each person more than once.

> **Tanvi:** Me gusta hacer surf y piragüismo.
>
> **Ali:** Me encanta nadar y tomar el sol.
>
> **Mario:** Quiero hacer excursiones y comprar recuerdos.
>
> **Daniela:** Prefiero visitar los pueblos y sacar fotos.

(a) .... likes to sunbathe. **(1 mark)**

(b) .... wants to buy souvenirs. **(1 mark)**

(c) .... likes to see the towns. **(1 mark)**

(d) .... wants to go canoeing. **(1 mark)**

(e) .... likes taking photos. **(1 mark)**

(f) .... enjoys a swim. **(1 mark)**

Listen to the recording

A typical holiday

2 Carlos is describing a typical holiday.

Listen to the recording and complete the sentences by putting a cross [×] in the correct box for each question.

(i) Carlos normally goes on holiday with his …

☐	**A**	girlfriend.
☐	**B**	family.
☐	**C**	friends.
☐	**D**	school.

(ii) Last year he spent most days …

☐	**A**	in the bar.
☐	**B**	in the games room.
☐	**C**	on the beach.
☐	**D**	at the pool.

(iii) In the afternoons he went …

☐	**A**	cycling.
☐	**B**	horse riding.
☐	**C**	fishing.
☐	**D**	sailing.

(iv) He ate …

☐	**A**	in the hotel.
☐	**B**	in the apartment.
☐	**C**	out.
☐	**D**	picnics on the beach.

(v) If the weather was bad they went …

☐	**A**	skating.
☐	**B**	bowling.
☐	**C**	rollerblading.
☐	**D**	shopping.

(5 marks)

Holiday experiences

An unforgettable experience

1   Read Guillermo's letter about his holiday.

> ¡Hola Ana!
>
> ¡Solo volvimos hace dos días pero quiero volver a México! Fueron las mejores dos semanas de mi vida y fue una experiencia maravillosa. Primero fuimos en avión a Nueva York y allí tuvimos que cambiar de aviones. Hubo un retraso de cinco horas debido a lluvias intensas en la Ciudad de México.
>
> Una vez allí, empezó la aventura y viajamos miles de kilómetros en el autocar con los otros viajeros, visitando varias ciudades y sitios de interés histórico. Las ruinas de los aztecas son fascinantes. Los últimos dos días nos alojamos en un hotel en la costa y nos relajamos, tomando el sol y nadando en el mar del Caribe. Una cosa que me sorprendió es que la playa es más grande de lo que parece en las fotos. ¡Y la comida mexicana es muy rica!.
>
> Un abrazo
> Guillermo

(i)   What does the letter tell us?

Put a cross [×] in each one of the **three** correct boxes.

A	He was a little disappointed with the holiday overall.	☐
B	They flew directly to Mexico City.	☐
C	Bad weather held up their flight.	☐
D	They stayed in one resort during the fortnight.	☐
E	They travelled with the rest of the tour party.	☐
F	Guillermo found the visits to the ruins a bit boring.	☐
G	For the last two days they were in a seaside resort.	☐

(3 marks)

Answer the following questions **in English**.

(ii)   What surprised him? ....   **(1 mark)**

(iii) What did he think of Mexican food? ....   **(1 mark)**

Holiday memories

2   Raquel is talking about her childhood holidays. Listen to the recording and put a cross [×] next to the **four** correct statements.

> Guided

Listen to the recording

A	The location was very noisy.	☐
B	Raquel enjoyed outdoor pursuits.	☐
C	The accomodation was luxurious.	☐
D	She never went on holiday alone.	☐
E	She stayed for a few days.	☐
F	She had fond memories of these holidays.	☐
G	She remembers the sights and sounds.	☐

> Note that, in this exercise, Raquel is talking about what she **used to** do when staying with her grandmother as a child. The action was recurring, so the verbs are in the imperfect tense. In exercise 1, the action was a one-off holiday in the past, so the preterite is used.

(4 marks)

Transport and directions

Guided

Directions to the flat

1 Read Saleh's email giving you directions to his flat.

Answer the following questions **in English**. You do not need to write in full sentences.

> ✉
>
> ¡Hola David!
>
> El jueves, cuando llegues a la estación, dobla a la derecha al salir y sigue todo recto hasta el río. Cruza el puente y toma la calle San Lorenzo – es la segunda calle a la izquierda. Al final de la calle, llegarás a la Plaza de la Iglesia; tienes que cruzarla y, después, sigue la calle con Correos a la derecha. Toma la tercera calle a la derecha y nuestro bloque de pisos está enfrente de la peluquería.
>
> Hasta pronto
>
> Saleh

(a) What should David do first on leaving the station? .... **(1 mark)**

(b) What should he do when he gets to the river? .... **(1 mark)**

(c) Where is San Lorenzo Street? .... **(1 mark)**

(d) What must he cross at the end of the street? .... **(1 mark)**

(e) What building is in the next street? .... **(1 mark)**

(f) Where is the block of flats? .... **(1 mark)**

> You do not need to answer in full sentences. As long as your answer makes sense and answers the question, that's all that is necessary.

Guided

Describing how you travel

2 Tu amiga Adriana te pregunta sobre cómo viajas.

Escribe una respuesta a Adriana.

> For the first bullet point you could show off some weather vocabulary instead of repeating the words given. You could start with 'Cuando hace sol …' and 'Cuando llueve …'.

Debes mencionar los puntos siguientes:

- cómo vas al instituto, con buen tiempo y con mal tiempo
- cómo prefieres viajar cuando vas de vacaciones
- cómo es el transporte en tu región
- cómo vas a viajar para hacer más ejercicio.

Escribe aproximadamente 80–90 palabras **en español**. Escribe la respuesta en una hoja de papel.

....

....

....

....

....

.... **(20 marks)**

Transport problems

Travel problems

Listen to the recording

1 Your friend Renato tells you about a terrible journey.

Listen to the recording and complete each sentence using a word from the box.
There are more words than gaps.

caught	three	close	crash	petrol	bus
breakdown	two	open	tickets	car	missed

(a) Renato was going to the station by .... **(1 mark)**

(b) First they had to go and get .... **(1 mark)**

(c) The hold-ups were due to a lorry .... **(1 mark)**

(d) Renato .... his train. **(1 mark)**

(e) Then there was a problem with one of the doors, which wouldn't .... **(1 mark)**

Role play: reporting an accident

Prepare your answers using the prompts. Then listen to the recording of the teacher's part and answer in the pauses. If you need more time, simply pause the recording. An example of a complete role play is recorded in the answer section.

Guided

Listen to the recording

2 You are telling the transport police about a road accident that you witnessed.
The teacher will play the part of the police officer and will speak first.

You must address the police officer as *usted*. You will talk to the teacher using the five prompts below.

Usted está hablando con un policía sobre un accidente que vio.

1 Su situación cuando vio el accidente

2 Qué pasó

3 !

4 ? Muchos accidentes allí

5 ? Número de personas en los coches

> You will need a combination of present, preterite and imperfect tenses: the imperfect to describe where you were and anything that was going on, the preterite for the events that you saw and the present for the first question you ask. Think carefully about which tense you might need to answer the unexpected question.

Holiday problems

Listen to the recording

[QR code]

Problems in the apartment

1 Señora Martínez is talking to the receptionist.

Listen to the recording and answer the questions **in English**.

(a) What exactly is the problem with the balcony?

.... **(1 mark)**

(b) What is her second complaint?

.... **(1 mark)**

(c) What is the cause of the problem?

.... **(1 mark)**

(d) What is wrong in the bathroom? Give **two** details.

.... **(2 marks)**

(e) Why does Señora Martínez like the apartment complex? Give **two** details.

.... **(2 marks)**

(f) How would she like to resolve the situation?

.... **(1 mark)**

Translation

2 Translate the following sentences **into Spanish.**

(a) The shower does not work.

> Guided

.... **(2 marks)**

(b) There are no sheets on the bed.

.... **(2 marks)**

(c) I need two towels in the bathroom.

.... **(2 marks)**

(d) I visited the town yesterday and I lost my passport.

.... **(3 marks)**

(e) The bathroom isn't very clean and the soap is missing.

.... **(3 marks)**

Because you are dealing with problems, you often need to make negative comments such as 'does **not** work' or 'there are **no** sheets'. Remember to make the verb negative by putting *no* in front: *Hay papel higiénico* = There is toilet paper. *No hay papel higiénico* = There isn't any toilet paper.

Asking for help abroad

Guided

Lost property

1 You see this notice in the window of your campsite in Menorca.

Lista de objetos encontrados

(8 – 15 de agosto)

Objeto	Número	Objeto	Número
llaves	6	toallas	7
paraguas	4	pendientes	8
gafas de sol	5	móviles	2
relojes	3		

Complete the gap in each sentence using a word or words from the box below.
There are more words than gaps.

books   cameras   earrings   keys   mobile phones   wallets

purses   sunglasses   towels   umbrellas   watches   sun hats

(a) There are 4 .... in the office.   **(1 mark)**

(b) There are 8 .... in the office.   **(1 mark)**

(c) There are 2 .... in the office.   **(1 mark)**

(d) There are 6 .... in the office.   **(1 mark)**

(e) There are 3 .... in the office.   **(1 mark)**

> It is essential to learn vocabulary as you go along, but you can sometimes use word similarities to help you understand. The word *móviles* is only one letter different from its English equivalent. *Paraguas* contains the word *agua*, so it can be linked to 'water' and therefore 'umbrellas'.

Reporting a robbery

2 You hear a woman reporting a robbery in a police station in Alicante.
Listen to the recording and answer the questions **in English.**

Listen to the recording

(a) Where was it when it was taken? ....   **(1 mark)**

(b) When did it happen? ....   **(1 mark)**

(c) How does she describe it? ....   **(1 mark)**

(d) What else might help the police to identify it? ....   **(1 mark)**

(e) What must she now do? ....   **(1 mark)**

Eating in a café

In the café

Listen to the recording

1 Some friends are ordering in a café in Murcia. What do they order?

Listen to the recording and put a cross [×] in each one of the **three** correct boxes.

A	a coffee with milk	☐
B	still water and a portion of omelette	☐
C	a strawberry ice cream	☐
D	a sandwich	☐
E	a vanilla ice cream	☐
F	an orange juice	☐
G	a hot dog	☐

(3 marks)

Role play: ordering in a café

Prepare your answers using the prompts. Then listen to the recording of the teacher's part and answer in the pauses. If you need more time, simply pause the recording. An example of a complete role play is recorded in the answer section.

⟩**Guided**⟩

Listen to the recording

2 You are with a Spanish friend in a café in Valencia and are ordering drinks and a snack. The teacher will play the part of your friend and will speak first.

You must address your friend as *tú*. You will talk to the teacher using the five prompts below.

Estás con tu amigo/a en una cafetería y pides algo para beber y comer.

1	Bebida – tipo	**4**	Opinión sobre la comida española
2	Algo para comer	**5**	? Precio
3	!		

> You need to learn how to ask what something costs: ask either ¿Cuánto es? or ¿Cuánto cuesta?

Friends in a café

3 Mandas esta foto de tu hermana y sus amigos a tu amigo español.

Describe la foto. Escribe aproximadamente 20–30 palabras **en español**.

....

....

....

....

....

....

(12 marks)

Eating in a restaurant

Eating out

1 You are eating out with friends in Madrid and they need your advice about the menu.

Menú del día	12 €	Incluido: Pan, vino y café
Entrantes	**Platos principales**	**Postres**
Espaguetis	Pollo	Melocotón
Ensalada	Bistec	Tarta de manzana
Sopa de tomate	Tortilla de patatas	Helado

What do you recommend to each friend? Write your answers **in English**.

(a) I want a cold starter. .... **(1 mark)**

(b) I'd like a vegetarian main course. .... **(1 mark)**

(c) I really like pasta. .... **(1 mark)**

(d) I just want fruit for dessert. .... **(1 mark)**

(e) I only eat white meat. .... **(1 mark)**

In a restaurant

2 You hear a man ordering for himself and his family in a restaurant. What does he ask the waitress about?

Listen to the conversation and put a cross [×] in each one of the **three** correct boxes.

Listen to the recording

A	what is included in the menu	☐
B	the fish dish	☐
C	what ingredients are in a dish	☐
D	smaller portions for children	☐
E	a dessert that is dairy free	☐
F	a recommendation for a wine	☐
G	the types of coffee available	☐

(3 marks)

Shopping for food

A shopping list

1 Read this note from your Spanish exchange partner's mother.

> **Hola chicos**
>
> ¿Podéis ir a las tiendas para comprarme estas cosas?
> He dejado dinero en la mesa de la cocina.
>
> **Mercado**
>
> medio kilo de plátanos
>
> un kilo de cebollas
>
> un pepino
>
> medio kilo de zanahorias
>
> **Supermercado**
>
> una docena de huevos grandes
>
> cuatro lonchas de jamón
>
> una caja de galletas (podéis escoger el tipo)
>
> una lata de alubias

Answer the following questions **in English.**

(a) Where has she left the money for the shopping? .... **(1 mark)**

(b) How many carrots should they get? .... **(1 mark)**

(c) Where should they get the onions? .... **(1 mark)**

(d) What fruit do they need to buy? .... **(1 mark)**

(e) What have they got to choose? .... **(1 mark)**

(f) How much ham should they get? .... **(1 mark)**

(g) What is the last item on the supermarket list? .... **(1 mark)**

Role play: going shopping

> Prepare your answers using the prompts. Then listen to the recording of the teacher's part and answer in the pauses. If you need more time, simply pause the recording. An example of a complete role play is recorded in the answer section.

> Guided

2 You are shopping for food in Tarragona. The teacher will play the part of the shop assistant and will speak first.

Listen to the recording

You must address the shop assistant as *usted.* You will talk to the teacher using the five prompts below.

Usted está comprando comida en una tienda en Tarragona. Habla con el dependiente / la dependienta.

1 Fruta – tipo

2 !

3 Algo para beber

4 Algo para poner en un bocadillo – cantidad

5 ? El precio

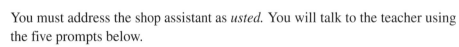

> Remember that the prompts will never provide you with the vocabulary you need, so when you are asked to order fruit, you must think of a type, such as *plátanos, manzanas* or *naranjas.*

Buying gifts

Listen to the recording

Comprando regalos

1 Oyes una conversación entre tus amigos españoles mientras estáis de compras.

Completa cada frase con una palabra del recuadro. Hay más palabras que espacios.

| variado | Navidad | librería | joyas | cumpleaños | ropa | biblioteca |

| centro comercial | barato | maquillaje | mercado | caramelos |

(a) Prefiere ir allí porque es más .... **(1 mark)**

(b) Quieren comprar regalos de .... **(1 mark)**

(c) Deciden que **no** van a comprar .... **(1 mark)**

(d) Piensan que lo ideal sería comprar .... **(1 mark)**

(e) Si les queda dinero, van a ir a la .... **(1 mark)**

> You will not hear the exact words in the box, but the vocabulary and phrases used in the recording will give you clues so that you can make the connection to the correct word.

Wrapping gifts

2 Your Spanish exchange partner's mother has left instructions for you both to wrap and label some Christmas presents for her nieces. Read her note.

Which present is for each person? Enter either **Elena**, **Marta**, **Lorena** or **Patricia**. You can use each name more than once.

> Elena: los guantes rojos y la barra de labios rosa
>
> Marta: el cinturón de cuero y los vaqueros negros
>
> Lorena: las zapatillas de deporte y el jersey de lana
>
> Patricia: el paraguas azul y el collar verde

(a) .... will get something made of wool. **(1 mark)**

(b) .... will receive some jewellery. **(1 mark)**

(c) .... will receive some make up. **(1 mark)**

(d) .... will receive a useful gift for rainy weather. **(1 mark)**

(e) .... will receive some gloves. **(1 mark)**

(f) .... will receive some footwear. **(1 mark)**

Opinions about food

European cuisine

1   Read this article about food in Europe.

> He pasado quince años viajando por Europa y escribiendo artículos para los periódicos sobre los platos que he probado. Mi conclusión es que la comida europea se destaca por la variedad enorme, no de los ingredientes usados, sino de los métodos de cocinar. Los cocineros de la gran mayoría de los países se esfuerzan mucho por utilizar los productos regionales en la temporada apropiada. Por eso, en las zonas costeras se ven muchos mariscos y donde hay campos verdes encontrarás queso de cabra y carne de vaca.
>
> Sin embargo, hay características nacionales notables que diferencian a los países. En Francia aprecian las salsas ricas en mantequilla, mientras que en Italia disfrutan más de los productos de alta calidad preparados simplemente. En Gran Bretaña siempre han sido populares las tartas y los pasteles, pero hoy en día también son populares una gran variedad de opciones más ligeras.

Put a cross [×] in the correct box for each question.

(i)   In Europe there is a lot of variety in …

☐	**A**	the produce they use.
☐	**B**	how they prepare the dishes.
☐	**C**	the way they grow the ingredients.
☐	**D**	the equipment used in the kitchen.

(ii) The chefs have in common that they …

☐	**A**	buy from local producers.
☐	**B**	import a lot of products from abroad.
☐	**C**	grow a lot of their own food.
☐	**D**	experiment with exotic ingredients.

(iii) What might you find in a rural area?

☐	**A**	sheep's cheese
☐	**B**	cream cheese
☐	**C**	blue cheese
☐	**D**	goat's cheese

(iv) Which country is said to prefer plainer food?

☐	**A**	France
☐	**B**	Italy
☐	**C**	Great Britain
☐	**D**	Spain

(v) Where do people often choose lighter meal options nowadays than in the past?

☐	**A**	France
☐	**B**	Italy
☐	**C**	Great Britain
☐	**D**	Spain

(5 marks)

Translation

> The translation task will always test more than one tense, so before you start read the text through and look out for tenses other than the present. Here, there are references to both the past and the future as well as the present.

2   Traduce el texto siguiente **al español**. Escribe la traducción en una hoja de papel.

> I like Spanish food a lot and the restaurant near the square makes really good food. The fish is very tasty and I loved the spicy sausage that I had last week. The food is always appetizing and, in my opinion, it is fairly healthy. We are going to eat there on Friday.

(12 marks)

The weather

El pronóstico del tiempo

1　Lee este boletín meteorológico para varias partes de España.

El tiempo para hoy

El sur: habrá temperaturas altas durante todo el día con la posibilidad de tormentas esta tarde y lluvias intensas en algunas zonas.

El este: un día caluroso y soleado para todos con temperaturas elevadas para la estación. El buen tiempo continuará varios días.

El norte: no hace frío pero será un día nublado con cielos cubiertos en todas partes. Posibilidades de niebla en zonas junto al mar.

El oeste: seco pero con vientos fuertes en algunas zonas. Temperaturas bajas todo el día.

¿Dónde viven estas personas? Escribe **sur**, **este**, **norte** o **oeste**.

(a)　Voy a llevar mi paraguas.　　.......................................　**(1 mark)**

(b)　Me pongo abrigo y guantes.　　.......................................　**(1 mark)**

(c)　Ideal para nadar en el mar.　　.......................................　**(1 mark)**

(d)　Es perfecto para el windsurf.　　.......................................　**(1 mark)**

(e)　No conduciré en la carretera de la costa.　.......................................　**(1 mark)**

Translation

2　Translate this passage **into English.**

> Vivo en el noroeste de España y el clima aquí no es tan caluroso como en el sur. En verano hace buen tiempo, pero el sol no brilla todos los días. Hemos tenido un fin de semana lluvioso.

> When you are translating, remember that you cannot always translate word for word, as it will produce some very odd-sounding English. Translating *todos los dias* literally would produce 'all the days', so you need to think for a moment and come up with a natural phrase such as 'every day'.

....

....

....

....

....

....　**(12 marks)**

Places to see

What to see in town

1 The woman in the tourist office is explaining what to see in the town.

Listen to the recording and answer the following questions **in English**.

Guided

Listen to the recording

(a) Where is the medieval castle? Give **two exact** details.

....

.... **(2 marks)**

(b) Why is the bullring particularly interesting?

.... **(1 mark)**

(c) How do we know the museum is award-winning?

.... **(1 mark)**

(d) What does the museum show?

.... **(1 mark)**

(e) Where is the modern art gallery?

.... **(1 mark)**

(f) Where is the chemist's?

.... **(1 mark)**

> If the question asks you to give details / exact details, you must produce a full answer. For example, if you hear *El museo está en la Plaza Mayor al lado de la biblioteca* and are asked to give exact details, you should write 'the museum is in the main square next to the library'.

Places to see

2 Mira la foto y prepara las respuestas a los siguientes puntos:

- la descripción de la foto
- tu opinión sobre visitar ciudades en otros países
- los sitios que los turistas visitan en tu región
- la ciudad donde más te gustaría vivir y por qué
- lo que visitaste en tus últimas vacaciones

Listen to the recording

> Prepare your answers using the prompts. Then listen to the recording of the teacher's questions and answer in the pauses. There is a recording of one student's answers in the answer section to give you more ideas.

Tourist information

In the tourist office

Listen to the recording

1   You hear a conversation between a customer and the assistant in the tourist office.

Listen to the recording and answer the following questions **in English**.

(a)   What does the assistant give him?

.... **(1 mark)**

(b)   Where is the tourist office situated?

.... **(1 mark)**

(c)   Where will he find the shops?

.... **(1 mark)**

(d)   What does he learn about the museum?

.... **(1 mark)**

(e)   What does the leaflet explain? Give **two exact** details.

....

.... **(2 marks)**

(f)   What does the assistant recommend?

.... **(1 mark)**

Role play: enquiries at the tourist office

> Prepare your answers using the prompts. Then listen to the recording of the teacher's part and answer in the pauses. If you need more time, simply pause the recording. An example of a complete role play is recorded in the answer section.

> Guided

Listen to the recording

2   You are making enquiries in a tourist office. The teacher will play the part of the employee and will speak first.

You must address the employee as *usted*. You will talk to the teacher using the five prompts below.

Usted está hablando con el empleado / la empleada de una oficina de turismo.

   1   Sitios de interés – información

   2   Alojamiento – lista

   3   **!**

   4   Transporte – horario

   5   **?** Estación – dónde

> Try to vary the language you use. For example, when asking for things you can alternate between *quiero*, *quisiera* and *me gustaría*.

Describing a town

⟨ **Guided** ⟩

Arriving in Sintra

1 Read this extract, adapted from *El Club Dumas* by Arturo Pérez Reverte.

> Corso estuvo en Lisboa menos de cincuenta minutos; el tiempo justo para ir de la estación de Santa Apolonia a la del Rossío. Hora y media más tarde pisaba el andén de Sintra bajo un cielo de nubes bajas que iluminaban las melancólicas torres grises del castillo Da Pena. No había taxis a la vista, y subió andando hasta el pequeño hotel situado enfrente de las dos grandes chimeneas del Palacio Nacional. Eran las diez de la mañana de un miércoles y la explanada estaba libre de turistas y autocares; no hubo problema en conseguir una habitación con vistas al paisaje verde y las mansiones con sus jardines centenarios cubiertas de hiedra.*

*hiedra = ivy

(i) What building did Corso see on arrival in Sintra?

☐	**A**	the royal palace
☐	**B**	the church towers
☐	**C**	the Da Pena castle
☐	**D**	the grey town hall roof

(ii) Why did he walk to the hotel?

☐	**A**	The taxis were all busy.
☐	**B**	He could not afford a taxi.
☐	**C**	He wanted the fresh air.
☐	**D**	There were no taxis around.

(iii) Where was the hotel?

☐	**A**	opposite the Palace
☐	**B**	next to the Palace
☐	**C**	behind the Palace
☐	**D**	in front of the Palace

(iv) What did Corso notice about the esplanade?

☐	**A**	It was full of people.
☐	**B**	There were coaches parked along it.
☐	**C**	It was fairly deserted.
☐	**D**	A few tourists were walking there.

(v) What could he see from his hotel window?

☐	**A**	old ivy-covered buildings
☐	**B**	age-old gardens
☐	**C**	sea and sky
☐	**D**	a flower park

(5 marks)

> There will be challenging questions on the Higher exam paper, like this literary extract, but don't be put off by the vocabulary that you don't know. You can gauge the overall meaning from the words that you do recognise and this is often enough to guide you to the correct answer.

Tu ciudad

2 Tu profesor te ha pedido escribir una descripción de la ciudad para la revista del instituto.

Debes mencionar los puntos siguientes:

- algo sobre la historia de tu ciudad
- la industria de hoy y dónde trabaja la gente
- la red de transporte
- los espacios verdes.

Escribe aproximadamente 80–90 palabras **en español**. Escribe la respuesta en una hoja de papel.

(20 marks)

Countries and nationalities

> Guided

Visiting tourists

1   Read this report about last year's tourism figures in Valencia.

> La mayoría de los turistas fueron visitantes nacionales de otras comunidades españolas, pero hemos visto un mayor número de otros viajeros de otros lugares que en los años anteriores. La región es popular con los holandeses pero nunca atrae a muchos daneses. No vinieron tantos alemanes como antes, pero había más japoneses que el año pasado. Los suecos suelen alojarse en el campo a varios kilómetros de la costa, mientras que los belgas siempre optan por hoteles junto a la playa.

Complete the gap in each sentence using a word from the box below.
There are more words than gaps.

> Belgian   Spanish   German   Swiss   foreign   Dutch   French
>
> Danish   Japanese   Greek   Swedish   Norwegian   Italian   Polish

(a)   There was an increased number of .... travellers.   **(1 mark)**

(b)   The region is popular with the ....   **(1 mark)**

(c)   The area never attracts many .... people.   **(1 mark)**

(d)   There were fewer .... visitors.   **(1 mark)**

(e)   The .... visitors tend to stay inland.   **(1 mark)**

(f)   The .... tourists stay close to the beach.   **(1 mark)**

> The questions are carefully written to give you clues to where in the text to find your answer. Look out for vocabulary that appears in the question, such as 'The region is popular with', which should send you to *La región es popular con* in the text. Read around the words carefully to find the correct answer. Be wary of negatives, however, because if the text said *La región **no** es popular con los holandeses*, you would have to look elsewhere for the answer.

At the language school

2   The students in the language school are introducing themselves. Where are they from?

Listen to the recording and put a cross [×] in each one of the **three** correct boxes.

Listen to the recording

A	Wales	☐	**E**	Scotland	☐
B	France	☐	**F**	Canada	☐
C	Ireland	☐	**G**	USA	☐
D	Russia	☐			

(3 marks)

Places to visit

Listen to the recording

What to visit

1   You ask the receptionist at your hotel about what to see in the area. Listen to the recording and complete the sentences by putting a cross [×] in the correct box.

(i)   In Oviedo he recommends …

☐	A	the parks and gardens.
☐	B	the historic areas.
☐	C	the modern shopping streets.
☐	D	the old market and statues.

(ii)   Gijón is …

☐	A	an expensive town.
☐	B	a walled city.
☐	C	on the coast.
☐	D	famous for its galleries.

(iii)   When you arrive in Avilés, it seems …

☐	A	quite ugly.
☐	B	very quiet.
☐	C	extremely modern.
☐	D	really green.

(iv)   Proaza is great for …

☐	A	hiring quad bikes.
☐	B	watching the cycling race.
☐	C	the city's bike lanes.
☐	D	a country bike ride.

(v)   Pravia is a good place for …

☐	A	walks by the river.
☐	B	riverside cafés.
☐	C	canoeing.
☐	D	boat trips.

(5 marks)

Mi ciudad

Guided

2   Tu amigo/a español/a te pregunta lo que se puede hacer en tu región.

Escribe un email a tu amigo/a. **Debes** mencionar los puntos siguientes:

- lo que hay en tu ciudad
- unas actividades que vais a hacer durante el día
- lo que se puede hacer por la noche
- una visita que puedes organizar.

Escribe aproximadamente 80–90 palabras **en español**.

> Always read the tasks in full before you start, so that you can plan what you are going to write. This way you will not end up repeating yourself and will use a greater variety of language.

....

....

....

....

....

....

....

(20 marks)

Describing a region

Listen to the recording

Granada

1   Your teacher is describing the area you will visit on your Spanish exchange.

Listen to the recording and complete the sentences using the words from the box.
There are more words than gaps.

fishing	coast	horse riding	desert	villages	countryside
city	snow	farming	island	mountains	deer

(a)   To the south is the ...., where you can find ....

     villages.   **(2 marks)**

(b)   Inland you will travel through the ...., where you

     will see ....   **(2 marks)**

(c)   You will drive through the .... on the day you

     go ....   **(2 marks)**

Role play: the area where I live

Prepare your answers using the prompts. Then listen to the recording of the teacher's part and answer in the pauses. If you need more time, simply pause the recording. An example of a complete role play is recorded in the answer section.

Guided

Listen to the recording

2   You are talking to your Spanish friend about where you live. The teacher will play the part of your friend and will speak first.

You must address your friend as *tú*. You will talk to the teacher using the five prompts below.

Estás hablando con tu amigo/a español/a sobre dónde vives.

1   Tu ciudad – descripción

2   Tu región – detalles históricos

3   **!**

4   **?** Región – industria

5   **?** Ciudad – número de habitantes

Had a go ☐   Nearly there ☐   Nailed it! ☐

School subjects

Likes and dislikes

1   Read the email from your Spanish friend telling you about her subjects at school.

> ¡Hola! Pronto tengo que decidir las asignaturas que voy a estudiar el año que viene. Sin duda continuaré con el inglés porque es muy útil en el mundo moderno, y también sé que quiero hacer informática. Es una asignatura muy práctica. Mucha gente dice que las ciencias son importantes pero para mí son aburridísimas. Las matemáticas son una posibilidad porque, para mi sorpresa, las encuentro bastante fáciles. En cambio, es seguro que voy a dejar la historia: es interesante pero siempre saco malas notas porque es tan difícil aprender todas las fechas.

Answer the following questions **in English**.

(a) Why will she carry on with IT? .... **(1 mark)**

(b) What does she think of science? .... **(1 mark)**

(c) How does she find maths? .... **(1 mark)**

(d) What is her opinion of history? .... **(1 mark)**

(e) Will she carry on with history? Give a reason. ....

.... **(1 mark)**

School subjects

> Prepare your answers using the prompts. Then listen to the recording of the teacher's questions and answer in the pauses. There is a recording of one student's answers in the answer section to give you more ideas.

Guided

Listen to the recording

2   Mira la foto y prepara las respuestas a los siguientes puntos:

- la descripción de la foto

- tu opinión de estudiar informática

- las asignaturas que te gustaban en el pasado

- planes para tus estudios en el futuro

- !

> Note the use of the imperfect tense in the third prompt because you are required to talk about what you **used to** like. Your answer should be in the same tense, for example: *Antes me interesaba ... Las clases eran ...*

School life

LISTENING TRACK 56

Guided

Listen to the recording

Parents' evening

1   You accompany your Spanish friend, Alejandro, and his parents to a parents' evening. What aspects of Alejandro's work is the teacher pleased with?

Listen to the recording and put a cross [×] in each one of the **three** correct boxes.

A	remembering his PE kit	☐
B	bringing everything he needs to class	☐
C	answering the teacher's questions	☐
D	paying attention in lessons	☐
E	meeting deadlines	☐
F	working well in a group	☐
G	involvement in extracurricular activities	☐

(3 marks)

> You won't always hear the exact phrase that you read in the options so, when you listen, be prepared to pick out statements that mean the same thing. The words 'general progress', as in the example, are not used in the recording but you will hear *éxito* (success) and *ningunos problemas* (no problems), indicating that his general progress is fine.

SPEAKING TRACK 57

Guided

Listen to the recording

Role play: talking about school

> Prepare your answers using the prompts. Then listen to the recording of the teacher's part and answer in the pauses. If you need more time, simply pause the recording. An example of a complete role play is recorded in the answer section.

2   Your Spanish friend is asking how you are getting on at school. The teacher will play the part of your friend and will speak first.

You must address your friend as *tú*. You will talk to the teacher using the five prompts below.

Estás hablando con tu amigo/a sobre tu instituto.

1   Deberes típicos – tipo

2   Actividades o clubes en el instituto

3   !

4   ? Uniforme – descripción

5   ? Exámenes recientes – ¿cómo?

> The unprepared question will be in keeping with the rest of the conversation so, during the preparation time, try to think what questions could logically be asked that are on the same topic but are not covered in the other points. You could jot down useful vocabulary as ideas come to you.

Had a go ☐　Nearly there ☐　Nailed it! ☐

The school day

Un día de colegio

1　Lee este email de tu amigo mallorquín que describe el día escolar.

Pon una cruz [×] en la casilla correcta.

> Las clases empiezan a las ocho, así que durante el invierno todavía es de noche cuando salimos de casa. Vamos en seguida a la primera clase, que ayer fue religión, seguida de física. Después de tres clases tenemos un descanso de media hora, y salimos al patio para charlar y comer un bocadillo que hemos traído de casa. Cada clase dura una hora y el día termina a las dos y media. A esa hora volvemos a casa para comer, y luego por la tarde hacemos los deberes. ¿Cómo es el horario en tu instituto?

(i)　Cuando dejan la casa en enero …

☐	**A**	no hay luz.
☐	**B**	cogen el autobús.
☐	**C**	se ponen el abrigo.
☐	**D**	hace frío.

(ii)　La segunda clase ayer fue …

☐	**A**	sociología.
☐	**B**	educación física.
☐	**C**	estudios religiosos.
☐	**D**	ciencia.

(iii)　A media mañana hay un corto …

☐	**A**	reunión.
☐	**B**	bocadillo.
☐	**C**	recreo.
☐	**D**	examen.

(iv)　A las dos y media …

☐	**A**	empieza la última clase.
☐	**B**	tienen un recreo.
☐	**C**	van a casa.
☐	**D**	hacen los deberes.

(v)　El amigo quiere saber …

☐	**A**	tu opinión de las clases.
☐	**B**	los detalles de tu día escolar.
☐	**C**	cómo vas al instituto.
☐	**D**	a qué hora te acuestas.

(5 marks)

Mi día en el instituto

2　You phone your Spanish friend, Paula, to ask about a typical day in her school. Listen to her reply and answer the questions **in English.**

(a)　What time does she leave home? .... **(1 mark)**

(b)　Where does she meet her friends? .... **(1 mark)**

(c)　How long is break? .... **(1 mark)**

(d)　Why don't they have school clubs? .... **(1 mark)**

(e)　Give **one** example of what they might do in the afternoon.

.... **(1 mark)**

Listen to the recording

Comparing schools

A visiting student

Listen to the recording

1 Pedro, a visiting student, is talking about the differences between your school and his. What aspects does he mention?

Listen to the recording and put a cross [×] in each one of the **three** correct boxes.

A	subjects	☐
B	teachers	☐
C	equipment	☐
D	extracurricular activities	☐
E	rules	☐
F	holidays	☐
G	uniform	☐

(3 marks)

Impressions of a British school

Guided

2 Read this article from a Spanish school magazine about a student's impressions of a British school.

> El centro escolar que visité es un típico instituto mixto de unos mil estudiantes. Lo primero que noté fue que empiezan a las nueve. En la carretera delante del instituto hay atascos y gente impaciente ya que todos los autobuses y los padres en sus coches llegan al mismo tiempo.
>
> A las nueve hay que ir a un aula para que el profe pase lista y luego van a las clases. Algunas asignaturas difieren de las nuestras, por ejemplo, se puede estudiar arte dramático y empresariales. Durante la hora de comer, sobre las doce y media (¡qué temprano!), van al comedor y toman un plato principal y un postre. Después, tienen dos horas más de clase antes de terminar el día a las tres y media. Igual que en España, tienen sus deberes cada día pero aquí suelen hacerlos después de cenar.

Answer the following questions **in English**.

(a) What was the first thing that he noticed? .... **(1 mark)**

(b) What did he see outside the school? .... **(1 mark)**

(c) Why did this happen? .... **(1 mark)**

(d) What started the school day? .... **(1 mark)**

(e) What **two** subjects would not be studied in Spain? .... **(2 marks)**

(f) What does he think about the timing of lunch? .... **(1 mark)**

(g) What similarity does he comment on? .... **(1 mark)**

> You can sometimes use your cultural knowledge to work out an answer. For question (d), you will find in the text that at 9 o'clock they go to a classroom *para que el profe pase la lista*. You can connect *lista* to the English word 'list', and from your own experience you know that first thing in the morning the teacher takes the register, which is a sort of list.

Describing schools

Guided

Saber perder by David Trueba

1 Read this extract.

Complete the sentences by putting a cross [×] in the correct box for each question.

> El Instituto Félix Paravicino se fundó en 1932, se amplió en 1967 con un impersonal edificio de hormigón que insulta su original belleza de ladrillo, y en 1985 pasó de femenino a mixto. En el edificio antiguo las escaleras son amplias. En el edificio nuevo las escaleras son estrechas, con reposamanos de pino barato barnizado en brillo. En el edificio viejo las ventanas son grandes, con dos hojas de madera y un cierre de hierro que gira con un roce agradable. En el edificio nuevo las ventanas son de aluminio, con un mango que cruje al accionarse.

(i) The school was founded in …

☐	**A**	1985.
☐	**B**	1967.
☐	**C**	1932.
☐	**D**	1931.

(ii) In the late sixties the school …

☐	**A**	was extended.
☐	**B**	was closed.
☐	**C**	received an award.
☐	**D**	burned down.

(iii) In the eighties …

☐	**A**	they introduced a uniform.
☐	**B**	there was a female head teacher.
☐	**C**	the pass rate was below average.
☐	**D**	it ceased to be a girls' school.

(iv) The stairs in the new building …

☐	**A**	lead to the staff room.
☐	**B**	are too steep.
☐	**C**	are narrow.
☐	**D**	are by the lift.

(v) The new windows …

☐	**A**	don't open.
☐	**B**	have metal frames.
☐	**C**	overlook the car park.
☐	**D**	are large.

(5 marks)

> With challenging reading passages, it helps to have a broad vocabulary in English too. The words *amplió* and *amplias* in the text can both be linked to the English word 'ample', which means 'good sized' and implies plenty of space. Knowing this can help you to answer two of the questions.

Guided

Translation

2 Traduce el texto siguiente **al español**.
Escribe la traducción en una hoja de papel.

> In the translation text below there are several adjectives. Your writing in Spanish will be much more accurate if you learn the rules about making adjectives agree.

> My school is quite old and has lots of classrooms, three laboratories and a gym. It is ten minutes from my house by foot. Five years ago they built a big library, which is very modern and has good facilities. Next year they are going to create new tennis courts.

(12 marks)

School rules

Las reglas en el nuevo instituto

1 Tu amiga española te muestra las reglas de su nuevo instituto.

━━━━ Las reglas del instituto ━━━━

Regla 1 Hay que llegar a tiempo todos los días y, si algún día llegas después de las ocho, debes presentarte a la oficina de recepción. Si estás ausente algún día, tienes que llevar una carta de los padres al volver a clase.

Regla 2 Todos los estudiantes tienen el deber de traer todo el material necesario para la clase. También se debe llevar la ropa apropiada.

Regla 3 No hay que llevar uniforme pero debes vestirte de una manera limpia y práctica. Las joyas representan un peligro en los laboratorios, así que están prohibidas.

Regla 4 No debéis llevar artículos de gran valor al instituto como auriculares, móviles y tabletas. Se pierden fácilmente y no los vas a necesitar en clase.

¿En qué regla está la respuesta? Escoge entre **Regla 1**, **Regla 2**, **Regla 3** o **Regla 4**. Puedes usar las frases más de una vez.

(a) ¿Puedo llevar mi ordenador? .... **(1 mark)**

(b) ¿Qué hago si llego tarde? .... **(1 mark)**

(c) ¿Y si pierdo clases por enfermedad? .... **(1 mark)**

(d) ¿Puedo llevar pendientes? .... **(1 mark)**

(e) ¿Necesito zapatillas cuando tenemos educación física? .... **(1 mark)**

Las reglas de mi instituto

2 Tu amigo español te ha preguntado sobre las reglas de tu instituto. Escribe un email a tu amigo. **Debes** mencionar los puntos siguientes:

- unas cosas que están prohibidas
- una regla que encuentras apropiada
- reglas sobre el comportamiento
- una regla que te parece tonta.

Justifica tus ideas y opiniones.

Escribe aproximadamente 130–150 palabras **en español**. Escribe la respuesta en una hoja de papel.

En mi instituto no se puede ....

....

....

....

....

....

....

.... **(28 marks)**

Problems at school

Guided

A forum about school

1 Read these entries on an online forum about the problems some students are facing at school.

Isabel	Acabamos de tener exámenes y el viernes pasado descubrí que suspendí casi todos. He perdido todo interés en el colegio y esta semana hice novillos. Es la primera vez que he hecho esto pero no tengo ningún entusiasmo por ir.
Saleh	No importa cuánto esfuerzo hago, no puedo sacar las notas que mis padres esperen. Paso horas repasando, he dejado de salir con mis amigos y no hago más que estudiar – nada, sólo saco un seis sobre diez.
Elisa	Elegí diseño gráfico como una de mis clases opcionales. Al principio me gustó mucho, pero ahora estoy empezando a aburrirme. No sé si debería cambiar a otra asignatura o darle un poco más de tiempo antes de decidir.
David	Todas mis hermanas hicieron ciencias y fueron a la universidad para estudiar medicina, como mi madre, o ingeniería. Detesto esas asignaturas y para mí son dificilísimas. ¿Cómo les puedo decir a mis padres que sólo me interesa la cocina?

Who says what about their school experience?

Enter either **Isabel**, **Saleh**, **Elisa** or **David** in the gaps below. Some names may be used twice or not at all.

(a) .... is feeling bored in a particular class.   **(1 mark)**

(b) .... has started skipping lessons.   **(1 mark)**

(c) .... has been working really hard.   **(1 mark)**

(d) .... feels pressured to follow in the family footsteps.   **(1 mark)**

Answer the following questions **in English**. You do not need to write in full sentences.

(e) How did Isabel do in the recent exams?

....   **(1 mark)**

(f) Which **two** career areas has David rejected?

....   **(1 mark)**

> Don't forget that all the texts you read provide opportunities to improve your own speaking and writing by borrowing useful phrases and a variety of ideas to extend your work.
> You could keep a notebook, divided into topic areas, in which to note down useful vocabulary.

Translation

2 Translate this passage **into English**. Complete the task on a separate piece of paper.

> Muchos estudiantes dicen que, en la sociedad moderna, hay un alto nivel de presión en los institutos. Piensan que sólo es aceptable sacar las mejores notas y estudiar las asignaturas más académicas. Algunos institutos han organizado sesiones después de las clases diseñadas para reducir el estrés. Estas incluyen la natación, el boxeo y un coro.

(12 marks)

Primary school

Listen to the recording

At primary school

1 Your Spanish friend tells you what he can remember about primary school.
What does he mention?

Listen to the recording and put a cross [×] in each one of the **three** correct boxes.

A	maths	☐
B	teachers	☐
C	toys	☐
D	playtime	☐
E	languages	☐
F	dinners	☐
G	uniform	☐

(3 marks)

Guided

Listen to the recording

Primary school

Prepare your answers using the prompts. Then listen to the recording of the teacher's questions and answer in the pauses. There is a recording of one student's answers in the answer section to give you more ideas.

2 Mira la foto y prepara las respuestas a los siguientes puntos:

- la descripción de la foto

- cómo eras cuando eras pequeño/a

- cómo era tu profesor favorito o profesora favorita

- las actividades que te gustaban más

- !

Don't be nervous about the imperfect tense, it's actually the most regular tense in Spanish! There are only three irregular verbs:

ser   (era, eras, era, éramos, erais, eran)

ir   (iba, ibas, iba, íbamos, ibais, iban)

ver   (veía, veías, veía, veíamos, veíais, veían)

Success in school

How to succeed

Listen to the recording

1   You are attending classes with your Spanish penfriend and listening to the teacher's advice. What is his message?

Listen to the recording and complete the sentences by putting a cross [×] in the correct box for each question.

(i)   You have to …

	A	attend all classes.
☐	**B**	read through the new work each day.
☐	**C**	relax at the end of the day.
☐	**D**	pack your bag when you go home.

(iv) If you miss a lesson, …

☐	**A**	check the lesson notes online.
☐	**B**	speak to the teacher next day.
☐	**C**	email school to let them know.
☐	**D**	get a study buddy to help.

(ii) You need to …

☐	**A**	report cases of bullying.
☐	**B**	leave things of value at home.
☐	**C**	ask questions as well as answer.
☐	**D**	avoid interrupting the teacher.

(v)   Success also depends on …

☐	**A**	a good attendance rate.
☐	**B**	getting help when you need it.
☐	**C**	doing lots of research.
☐	**D**	the standard of teaching.

(iii) It is advisable to …

☐	**A**	look out for study opportunities.
☐	**B**	balance study and leisure.
☐	**C**	do the hardest homework first.
☐	**D**	organise your homework diary.

(5 marks)

Role play: being a better student

> Prepare your answers using the prompts. Then listen to the recording of the teacher's part and answer in the pauses. If you need more time, simply pause the recording. An example of a complete role play is recorded in the answer section.

> **Guided**

Listen to the recording

2   You are talking to your Spanish friend about how to be successful in school. The teacher will play the part of your friend and will speak first.

You must address your friend as *tú*. You will talk to the teacher using the five prompts below.

Estás hablando con tu amigo/a de cómo tener éxito en el instituto.

1   Deberes – recomendación

2   Estudiante ideal – conducta en clase

3   **!**

4   Exámenes – preparación

5   **?** Repaso – cómo

> Question words are used a lot in role plays, so learning them thoroughly will help you. For example, if you are prompted to ask for a reason (*razón*) you will need to ask the question *¿por qué?* (why?). Here, remember that *cómo* means 'how' and can be used in your question.

School trips

Our day out

1 Carolina and her friends are talking about their school trips. Where have they been?

Listen to the recording and put a cross [×] in each one of the **three** correct boxes.

Guided

Listen to the recording

A	Roman villa	☐
B	art gallery	☐
C	factory	☐
D	university	☐
E	bank	☐
F	abroad	☐
G	cinema	☐

(3 marks)

> Listen to the recording twice before you write your answer, to avoid making a mistake that you then have to cross out. As you listen for the first time, you could jot down 'C', 'M' or 'B' in the space next to the lines. The second time round, make your final decision and write the answer you think is correct. In the exam, make sure that you leave just one clear answer to be marked.

Una excursión con el instituto

2 Tu profesor te ha pedido escribir un artículo para la revista escolar sobre una visita que hiciste con el instituto.

Escribe el artículo.

Debes mencionar los puntos siguientes:

- adónde fuiste
- cómo viajaste
- una actividad que hiciste
- tu opinión de la visita y por qué.

Escribe aproximadamente 80–90 palabras **en español**.

(20 marks)

....

....

....

....

....

....

....

....

....

....

School events

The yearly review

1 Read the head teacher's review of events at the school.

INFORME DE LA DIRECTORA

Este año hemos tenido un programa de eventos muy variado. En otoño, el departamento de música organizó un concurso de bandas que fue muy popular con los alumnos de todas las edades. Para Navidad tuvimos un espectáculo de baile, y para celebrar el final del trimestre hubo una fiesta con música de discoteca.

En primavera tuvimos mucho éxito en los deportes, ganando un campeonato de rugby y organizando un torneo de tenis para todos los colegios de la región.

Este trimestre vamos a presentar una obra de teatro y los jóvenes actores están preparándose desde hace siete meses. Sin duda será fenomenal.

Answer the following questions **in English**.

(a) When did the music department organise their event?

.... **(1 mark)**

(b) What was popular with students of all ages?

.... **(1 mark)**

(c) When was the dance show?

.... **(1 mark)**

(d) What sporting event did the school win?

.... **(1 mark)**

(e) How long have the students been rehearsing for the play?

.... **(1 mark)**

School events

> Prepare your answers using the prompts. Then listen to the recording of the teacher's questions and answer in the pauses. There is a recording of one student's answers in the answer section to give you more ideas.

Guided

Listen to the recording

2 Mira la foto y prepara las respuestas a los siguientes puntos:

- la descripción de la foto
- actividades deportivas en tu instituto
- un evento cultural en el colegio
- un evento que te gustaría tener en el instituto
- una actividad en que tú has participado

> As well as describing exactly what you see (orchestra, instruments) you can also make assumptions based on what you see. For example, here you could suggest that the students have been practising for many months and the teacher is very pleased with them.

School exchanges

The exchange programme

1 Read this programme for your school's Spanish exchange trip.

Answer the following questions **in English**.

Fechas:	marzo 20–27
Transporte:	avión y autocar
Ciudad:	Martorell, a treinta kilómetros de Barcelona
Alojamiento:	con una familia española

Programa:
· participación en clases
· visita a los monumentos principales de Barcelona
· excursión a la pista de hielo
· cena de despedida en un restaurante

(a) How will you be travelling? .... **(2 marks)**

(b) Where is Martorell? .... **(1 mark)**

(c) Where will you stay? .... **(1 mark)**

(d) What will you do in the school? .... **(1 mark)**

(e) What sporting activity is planned? .... **(1 mark)**

> It is important to know your numbers well, as it is very easy to confuse numbers such as *tres* (three), *trece* (thirteen) and *treinta* (thirty).

Opinions of an exchange

2 Your Spanish friend tells you about an exchange visit he went on last year.

Listen to the recording. Put a cross [×] in the **two** correct boxes for each question.

Listen to the recording

(i) He thought the exchange was worthwhile because …

A	he went out with an English girl.	☐
B	his exam grades improved.	☐
C	he got much better at speaking English.	☐
D	he learned so much about the lifestyle.	☐
E	he attended many cultural events.	☐

(2 marks)

(ii) He had problems with …

A	the food.	☐
B	mealtimes.	☐
C	going to bed so early.	☐
D	finding his way around.	☐
E	understanding rapid speech.	☐

(2 marks)

Future plans

Plans for the future

Guided

1 Read these plans on a website forum.

Verónica	Cuando deje el instituto, encontraré un trabajo interesante y variado que pague bien. Los jefes estarán tan impresionados conmigo que me darán varios ascensos, y después de cinco años viviré en un piso de lujo y tendré un coche deportivo y vacaciones en el Caribe.
Marcos	Primero iré a la universidad y cuando termine mi carrera, buscaré trabajo en el extranjero. Con mi experiencia de otras lenguas y culturas conseguiré empleo escribiendo para un periódico, y un día todo el mundo me conocerá como presentador de televisión.
Adrián	Soy un chico tradicional de una familia muy feliz y quiero repetir esa experiencia en el futuro. Cuando empiece a ganar un sueldo apropiado me casaré con mi novia y tendremos hijos. Viviremos en una pequeña casa en las afueras de la ciudad.
Lucía	Me interesa todo sobre los océanos, así que viajaré por el mundo en un barco. No tendré un trabajo de oficina. Pasaré el tiempo ayudando en proyectos de conservación de los océanos y recogiendo información sobre la vida marina. ¡Qué sueño más bonito!

Who says what about their future plans? Enter either **Verónica**, **Marcos**, **Adrián** or **Lucía**.
You can use each person more than once.

(a) .... will marry and have children. **(1 mark)**

(b) .... will **not** work indoors. **(1 mark)**

(c) .... wants to own expensive things. **(1 mark)**

(d) .... plans to help with
environmental problems. **(1 mark)**

(e) .... wants to achieve fame. **(1 mark)**

(f) .... does **not** talk about travel. **(1 mark)**

Las ambiciones de los jóvenes

2 Escuchas un programa de radio sobre las ambiciones de los jóvenes.

¿Qué dice el programa? Escoge entre **pocos**, **todos**, **muchos** o **ninguno**.
Puedes usar palabras más de una vez.

Listen to the recording

(a) ¿Cuántos jóvenes esperaban casarse? .... **(1 mark)**

(b) ¿Cuántos jóvenes querían trabajos motivadores? .... **(1 mark)**

(c) ¿Cuántos jóvenes aspiraban a ser famosos? .... **(1 mark)**

(d) ¿Cuántos jóvenes se preocupaban por el dinero? .... **(1 mark)**

(e) ¿Cuántos estudiantes esperaban tener una relación estable? .... **(1 mark)**

Future education plans

Guided

Options at 16

1 Read this extract from a Spanish school's careers guide.

> The text is addressing the students of the school, so it uses the second person plural form of address – 'you' familiar plural.

Al final de este curso vais a terminar la enseñanza secundaria y empezar una nueva fase en la vida. Este es el momento de tomar decisiones para el futuro. Muchos de vosotros vais a continuar con los estudios aquí en el instituto y tenéis que decidir las asignaturas que queréis hacer. Naturalmente, tendréis en cuenta los trabajos que os interesen, pero igualmente importante es que os gusten las asignaturas que escojáis.

Algunos de vosotros seguiréis cursos de formación profesional y hay que investigar bien los cursos disponibles antes de elegir la mejor opción para vuestra personalidad y habilidades.

También existe el mundo del trabajo, pero si preferís seguir esta ruta, es mejor buscar un aprendizaje con una compañía de confianza donde podáis aprender y ganar títulos además de recibir un sueldo.

Put a cross [✗] in the correct box for each question.

(i) If they are staying on, they must …

☐	A	decide what courses to follow.
☐	B	enrol as soon as possible.
☐	C	bring a letter of confirmation from home.
☐	D	pass all their subjects this year.

(ii) When choosing which subjects to take …

☐	A	think only of your future career plans.
☐	B	enjoyment of the subjects is vital.
☐	C	listen to advice from all sides.
☐	D	pick some new ones for variety.

(iii) For vocational courses you should …

☐	A	be prepared to travel.
☐	B	be aware of the cost of equipment.
☐	C	investigate the job openings in each area.
☐	D	look for one that suits you as an individual.

(iv) With which type of company should you seek work?

☐	A	reliable
☐	B	local
☐	C	big
☐	D	well-known

(v) Why is an apprenticeship recommended?

☐	A	The job prospects are better.
☐	B	You gain qualifications.
☐	C	The wages are good.
☐	D	It's a secure job.

(5 marks)

Listen to the recording

Plans for the future

2 Your exchange partner is talking about her plans for the next few years. What options is she considering?

Listen to the recording and put a cross [✗] in each of the **three** correct boxes.

A	getting an apprenticeship at 18	☐
B	getting a degree	☐
C	working in the travel industry	☐
D	taking a year out	☐
E	carrying on with languages	☐
F	looking for part-time work	☐
G	studying sciences	☐

(3 marks)

Using languages

Why study languages?

1 Some Spanish friends are discussing a careers talk they have just attended. What have they learned about the benefits of studying languages?

Listen to the recording and put a cross [×] in each one of the **four** correct boxes.

Listen to the recording

A	more job opportunities	☐
B	more employable if you've lived abroad	☐
C	essential for work in tourist industry	☐
D	can earn higher wage	☐
E	improve command of own language	☐
F	business lost by companies without foreign language speakers	☐
G	chance to work abroad	☐

(4 marks)

Translation

2 Translate this passage **into English.**

> Estudiar español puede abrirte muchas puertas a nivel profesional. Hay muchos países que tienen el español como lengua oficial, y por eso hay muchos puestos de trabajo en que hablar el idioma puede ser un factor fundamental. Saber hablar castellano puede ayudarte a disfrutar de la literatura y el cine. Empecé a aprender español hace dos años.

....

....

....

....

....

....

....

....

....

.... **(12 marks)**

> We use the articles (a/an/the) differently in Spanish and English and you will need to tackle them carefully when translating. The phrase *a nivel profesional* has no article in Spanish but will need 'a' in English. The phrase *como lengua oficial* is similar.

Jobs

A jobs forum

1 Read these entries on a forum from people who have changed their career path.

Ana	Después de ser soldado durante siete años, acabo de empezar la formación para ser bombera. Será un trabajo peligroso pero útil.
Juan	Me gustaba ser enfermero pero ahora que tengo un hijo no quiero trabajar de noche. Por eso, de momento trabajo como cajero por las mañanas.
Carlos	Estudio para ser farmacéutico y el curso termina este año. Empecé mis estudios con la ambición de ser médico pero cambié de opinión.
Laura	Cuando era joven quería ser diseñadora de moda pero ahora uso mis habilidades creativas en la arquitectura.

Who says what about their career? Enter either **Ana**, **Juan**, **Carlos** or **Laura**.
You can use each person more than once.

(a) .... switched degree courses.   **(1 mark)**

(b) .... handles money as part of the job.   **(1 mark)**

(c) .... has left a military career.   **(1 mark)**

(d) .... no longer wants to work late hours.   **(1 mark)**

(e) .... had different aspirations as a child.   **(1 mark)**

(f) .... has to consider family commitments.   **(1 mark)**

> As well as expressions of time, such as *ahora* (now) and *de momento* (at the moment), it is important to pay attention to the tenses used in order to be clear about when the events are taking place.

Pablo's family

2 Your Spanish friend, Pablo, is telling you about his family and their jobs.

Listen to the recording and complete the sentences. There are more words than gaps.

Listen to the recording

receptionist	police officer	shop assistant	secretary
waiter	teacher	mechanic	plumber	journalist
postal worker	builder	sales person

(a) Luis wanted to be a .... but can only find work as a ....   **(2 mark)**

(b) Pablo's father used to be a .... but starts a new job on Monday
as a ....   **(2 marks)**

(c) Manolo is a .... but his dream is to be a ....   **(2 marks)**

Opinions about jobs

Guided

Listen to the recording

Opiniones sobre los trabajos

1 Estás escuchando a tu amigo que está hablando de unos posibles trabajos.

¿Cuál es su opinión? Escoge entre **mal pagado**, **bien pagado**, **interesante** o **aburrido**. Puedes usar palabras más de una vez.

> To help you narrow down the options for the answers, listen out for words that are linked to pay. Do you hear any of the following: *euros* (euros), *dinero* (money), *ganar* (to earn), *pagar* (to pay), *sueldo* (wage), *salario* (salary)?

(a) Ser carpintero es un trabajo .... **(1 mark)**

(b) El trabajo de cartero le parece .... **(1 mark)**

(c) Trabajar en una tienda es un empleo .... **(1 mark)**

(d) Ser informático sería un trabajo .... **(1 mark)**

(e) El trabajo de cocinero es un empleo .... **(1 mark)**

Guided

Listen to the recording

Role play: talking about jobs

2 You are talking to your exchange partner about possible jobs.

The teacher will play the role of your exchange partner and will speak first.

You must address your friend as *tú*. You will talk to the teacher using the five prompts below.

> Prepare your answers using the prompts. Then listen to the recording of the teacher's part and answer in the pauses. If you need more time, simply pause the recording. An example of a complete role play is recorded in the answer section.

Estás hablando con tu amigo/a sobre distintos trabajos.

1 Aspectos importantes del trabajo

2 Trabajo menos preferido y razón

3 !

4 Trabajo ideal y razón

5 ? Importancia del dinero en el trabajo

> In role plays, you are often required to ask someone for an opinion, so it is a good idea to learn these phrases to start off your question: *¿Piensas que ...?, ¿Crees que ...?* (Do you think that ...?). A stylish way of asking the same thing is *¿Te parece que ...?*

Applying for jobs

Going for interview

1   Read this extract, adapted from the play *El Método Grönholm* by Jordi Galcerán.

> **ENRIQUE:** Y las condiciones son increíbles. El sueldo es... Bueno, no sé qué debes ganar tú, pero yo casi doblaría... Me preocupaba llegar tarde. Estas cosas son importantes. A veces, son los pequeños detalles los que inducen a tomar una decisión. Yo he contratado gente y, al final, lo que me lleva a decidir son los pequeños detalles. La manera de vestir, la forma cómo me han dado la mano... Y el coche. Siempre que puedo los acompaño hasta su coche. Un coche dice mucho de su propietario... Un coche, habla. A veces te encuentras con un tipo que parece muy aseado* y tiene el coche lleno de basura.

*aseado = neat and tidy

Answer the questions **in English**.

(a) If Enrique gets the job, how much will he earn? .... **(1 mark)**

(b) Apart from someone's car, what are the **two** other important little details, according to Enrique?

....

.... **(2 marks)**

(c) After interviewing someone, what does he always do if he can?

.... **(1 mark)**

(d) Why does he do this?

.... **(1 mark)**

(e) What has he sometimes found with an apparently neat and tidy person?

.... **(1 mark)**

Translation

2   Traduce el texto siguiente **al español**. Escribe la traducción en una hoja de papel.

> I am creative, hard-working and ambitious and I get on well with other people. I have experience as a waiter in a restaurant and I have worked as a receptionist in a hotel. I speak Spanish and a little French and I understand the importance of good relationships with the customers. The job would be ideal for me.

> Make sure you understand the difference between 'I have' when it means 'I own' or 'I possess' and 'I have' when it is part of a longer verb such as 'I have worked'. The former will be *tengo* and the latter will be *he trabajado*.

Guided

....

....

....

.... **(12 marks)**

67

Work experience

Carmen's work experience

1 Carmen is talking about her work experience. What does she mention?

Listen to the recording and put a cross [×] in each one of the **four** correct boxes.

Listen to the recording

A	the other employees	☐
B	her journey to work	☐
C	how long she worked	☐
D	disadvantages of this kind of work	☐
E	her ambitions	☐
F	the uniform she had to wear	☐
G	what she wants to do in the future	☐

(4 marks)

A forum on work experience

2 Read the opinions about work experience on a school website.

> **Pablo**
> Ayudaba a las enfermeras y servía la comida a los pacientes.
>
> **Javier**
> Leía historias a los niños más pequeños y ayudaba a los mayores con sus estudios.
>
> **Andrea**
> Organizaba las reservas de las habitaciones y daba las llaves a los clientes.
>
> **Rosa**
> Limpiaba y quitaba las mesas, y preparaba algunos de los platos más fáciles.

Answer the questions **in English.**

(a) Where did Pablo work? .... **(1 mark)**

(b) Where did Javier work? .... **(1 mark)**

(c) Where did Andrea work? .... **(1 mark)**

(d) Where did Rosa work? .... **(1 mark)**

Volunteering

Reasons to volunteer

1 Read what these young people say about why you should volunteer.

Alex	Simplemente para ayudar a los más necesitados. Es la primera razón por la que todos hacen actividades voluntarias, pero no es la única.
Begoña	No sólo te sientes bien ayudando a los demás, también sentirás cómo las personas a las que ayudas o los compañeros que conoces te valorarán por tu esfuerzo.
Carlos	Para cuidar el medio ambiente. No sólo existe el voluntariado para ayudar a las personas, sino también a la naturaleza.
Daniela	Para aprender a relacionarte. En el voluntariado conocerás a gente nueva, y si tienes problemas con las relaciones personales, te ayudará a llevarte mejor con tus compañeros. Aprenderás a trabajar de forma eficaz en grupo.

Who says what about volunteering?

Enter either **Alex**, **Begoña**, **Carlos** or **Daniela**. Some names may be used twice or not at all.

(a) .... states that you can get involved in helping wildlife. **(1 mark)**

(b) .... suggests you can improve interpersonal skills. **(1 mark)**

(c) .... points out how you will feel about yourself. **(1 mark)**

(d) .... outlines the benefits in developing your teamwork. **(1 mark)**

Guided

Listen to the recording

Volunteering

2 Mira la foto y prepara las respuestas a los siguientes puntos:

- la descripción de la foto

- beneficios del trabajo voluntario

- oportunidades en tu ciudad

- tu experiencia del trabajo voluntario

- qué ganaste con la experiencia

> Prepare your answers using the prompts. Then listen to the recording of the teacher's questions and answer in the pauses. There is a recording of one student's answers in the answer section to give you more ideas.

Helping others

Helping friends

1 Some Spanish friends are talking about how they have helped friends. How did they help?

Listen to the recording and put a cross [×] in each one of the **three** correct boxes.

Listen to the recording

A	helping with a fitness regime	☐
B	solving romantic problems	☐
C	intervening in a bullying issue	☐
D	lending money	☐
E	helping with studies	☐
F	giving a lift	☐
G	supporting after a family break-up	☐

(3 marks)

Helping at home

2 Publicas esta foto para tus amigos en tu página de una red social.

> You will need the phrase *lavar los platos* (to wash the dishes). You could also use the phrase *secar los platos* (to dry the dishes).

Describe la foto y da tu opinión sobre ayudar en casa.

Guided

Escribe aproximadamente 20–30 palabras **en español**.

....

....

....

....

(12 marks)

Charities

Charity events

Listen to the recording

1   You are at your Spanish penfriend's school, listening to a report from the head of the student charity group.

What does she say?

Listen to the recording and complete the sentences by putting a cross [×] in the correct box for each question.

(i)   They raised eighty euros …

☐	**A** for orphaned children.
☐	**B** for war veterans.
☐	**C** for endangered wildlife.
☐	**D** for homeless pets.

(ii)   The Christmas event …

☐	**A** took place at the hospital.
☐	**B** was a quiz for parents.
☐	**C** was in aid of needy families.
☐	**D** involved nine teams.

(iii)   The cakes …

☐	**A** went on sale at break.
☐	**B** were on a stall at the summer fete.
☐	**C** did not turn out to be very popular.
☐	**D** were a bit expensive to make.

(iv)   The environmental charity received a cheque for …

☐	**A** 50 euros.
☐	**B** 100 euros.
☐	**C** 110 euros.
☐	**D** 150 euros.

(v)   For the children's charity they will be collecting …

☐	**A** things to wear.
☐	**B** things to eat.
☐	**C** things to play with.
☐	**D** things to draw and paint with.

(5 marks)

Role play: charity events

Guided

Listen to the recording

2   You are talking to your Spanish friend, who has asked what charity events your school organises.

The teacher will play the part of your friend and will speak first.

> Prepare your answers using the prompts. Then listen to the recording of the teacher's part and answer in the pauses. If you need more time, simply pause the recording. An example of a complete role play is recorded in the answer section.

You must address your friend as *tú*. You will talk to the teacher using the five prompts below.

Estás hablando con tu amigo/a sobre los eventos benéficos en tu instituto.

1   Asociaciones – cuáles
2   Actividades – descripción
3   !
4   ? Su instituto – eventos
5   ? Organización benéfica favorita – razón

> You might not always be able to tell the truth in these exercises! Here, perhaps your school doesn't get involved in charity events or you can't remember. Your aim is to show off your knowledge of Spanish so, as long as your answer is reasonable (for example, you wouldn't claim to have made a million euros from a cake sale!), that is fine. You can get inspiration from exercise 1 or from the Revision Guide.

Careers and training

A letter of enquiry

1   Read the letter below.

> Estimada Señora Ondo:
>
> Me dirijo a usted para preguntarle la mejor manera de encontrar trabajo en el campo tecnológico.
>
> Me interesa el trabajo de técnico informático porque me gusta la idea de poder resolver los problemas tecnológicos de una compañía y crear soluciones para mejorar sus sistemas. Hasta el momento he estudiado informática hasta el nivel de bachillerato, pero ahora quiero saber la mejor forma para continuar.
>
> No sé si quiero seguir estudiando en la universidad, y me gustaría saber si hay cursos de formación más cortos para obtener títulos aceptados en la industria. Sería difícil hacer un internado de varios meses sin ganar nada de dinero, pero ¿piensa que me daría una gran ventaja a la hora de buscar trabajo fijo?
>
> Una última pregunta: ¿Dónde es el mejor sitio para buscar anuncios de trabajo en esta profesión?
>
> Espero que pueda ayudarme con estas preguntas y quedo a su disposición.
>
> Le saluda atentamente
>
> *Leticia Muñoz*
>
> Leticia Muñoz

Answer the following questions **in English**.

(a) What job is Leticia interested in? ....   **(1 mark)**

(b) Why does she want the job? Give **two** reasons. ....

....   **(2 marks)**

(c) What qualification does she have? ....   **(1 mark)**

(d) What alternative to university does she ask about?

....   **(1 mark)**

(e) Why is she concerned about an internship?

....   **(1 mark)**

(f) What is her final question?

....   **(1 mark)**

Planning for the future

2   Your Mexican friend, Álvaro, is telling you his plans. What does he mention?
    Listen to the recording and put a cross [×] in each one of the **three** correct boxes.

Listen to the recording

A	his experience of school	☐
B	gaining work experience	☐
C	studying science	☐
D	the subject he wants to teach	☐
E	his university friends	☐
F	how much he will earn	☐
G	the length of the training	☐

(3 marks)

Messages

Talking on the phone

Listen to the recording

1   You are trying to contact your Spanish friend, who is working on a campsite during the holidays. You phone the reception.

Answer the following questions in English.

(a) What does he ask you to do? ....   **(1 mark)**

(b) What must you do now? ....   **(1 mark)**

(c) What do you need now and why? ....   **(1 mark)**

(d) What is your friend's number? ....   **(1 mark)**

(e) What does he ask you? ....   **(1 mark)**

Messages from friends

2   Read these texts from Spanish friends.

Adrián

Te he mandado un correo electrónico. Mira el sitio web que te recomendé.

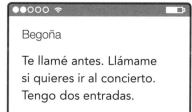

Begoña

Te llamé antes. Llámame si quieres ir al concierto. Tengo dos entradas.

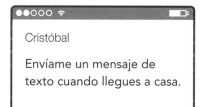

Cristóbal

Envíame un mensaje de texto cuando llegues a casa.

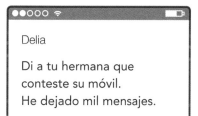

Delia

Di a tu hermana que conteste su móvil. He dejado mil mensajes.

Who leaves what message? Enter either **Adrián**, **Begoña**, **Cristóbal** or **Delia**. You can use each person more than once.

(a) .... wants to know if you got home safely.   **(1 mark)**

(b) .... wants you to tell someone to pick up the phone.   **(1 mark)**

(c) .... has tried to call you.   **(1 mark)**

(d) .... wants you to check out something on the internet.   **(1 mark)**

(e) .... needs you to phone them back.   **(1 mark)**

(f) .... has something you might want.   **(1 mark)**

Part-time jobs

> Guided

Listen to the recording

Weekend jobs

1 Some Spanish friends are talking about their part-time jobs. Where do they work?

Listen to the recording and put a cross [×] in each one of the **three** correct boxes.

A	drive-in restaurant	☐
B	hairdresser's	☐
C	newsagent's	☐
D	sweet shop	☐
E	garden centre	☐
F	bar	☐
G	home for the elderly	☐

(3 marks)

> Beware: in this type of question there are often red herrings! Rubén mentions 'customers' and 'food' and it would be easy to assume that he works in a bar. However, his last point is that many of the customers are in their car.

Listen to the recording

Role play: talking about part-time work

2 You are talking to your Spanish friend about your part-time job. The teacher will play the role of your friend and will speak first.

You must address your friend as *tú*. You will talk to the teacher using the five prompts below.

Estás hablando con tu amigo español / tu amiga española sobre tu trabajo a tiempo parcial.

1 Trabajo – dónde y cuándo

2 !

3 Tu opinión del trabajo

4 ? Su trabajo – viaje – cómo

5 ? Su trabajo – sueldo

> Prepare your answers using the prompts. Then listen to the recording of the teacher's part and answer in the pauses. If you need more time, simply pause the recording. An example of a complete role play is recorded in the answer section.

Money

Young people and money

1 Read the article below.

Los resultados indican que cerca del 70% de los menores y adolescentes reciben su paga en efectivo* para que realicen sus propias compras. Este dinero lo obtienen de sus padres en la mayoría de los casos, pero también de otros familiares.

"Esto sugiere que hay hogares en los cuales los niños reciben dinero de varias fuentes, lo cual ha aumentado en más del 50% la cantidad que reciben en comparación con otros tiempos", señaló Leonardo Ortegón, uno de los autores del estudio.

Según la investigación, los productos en los que más invierten su dinero son: las actividades de entretenimiento (22%), los alimentos y bebidas (21%) y los servicios de comunicación de telefonía celular (19%) e Internet (18%).

El estudio, además, concluye que el gasto per cápita por niño ha aumentado en las familias bogotanas**. Los padres y especialmente los abuelos están comprando más productos para sus hijos, en parte debido a que tienen mayores ingresos para gastar en estos artículos, pero también porque son presionados por ellos mismos para aumentar su consumo.

efectivo = cash
**bogotanas* – from Bogotá, the capital of Colombia

Answer the following questions **in English.**

(a) From whom do young people receive their pocket money?

.... **(1 mark)**

(b) What is said about the amount they receive?

.... **(1 mark)**

(c) What do they spend the largest percentage of their money on?

.... **(1 mark)**

(d) Why has spending on children gone up in families?

.... **(1 mark)**

Role play: talking about money

2 You are talking to your Spanish exchange partner about money. The teacher will play the role of your exchange partner and will speak first.

You must address your partner as *tú*. You will talk to the teacher using the five prompts below.

Estás hablando con tu amigo/a sobre el dinero.

1 Paga – cuánto

2 Paga – de quién y cuándo

3 **!**

4 Dinero – tus gastos

5 **?** Paga – bastante

> Prepare your answers using the prompts. Then listen to the recording of the teacher's part and answer in the pauses. If you need more time, simply pause the recording. An example of a complete role play is recorded in the answer section.

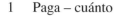

> Remember that asking Spanish questions is easy. To ask the question 'Do you receive enough pocket money?' you just say 'you receive' (*recibes*), add the words for 'enough' and 'money' and put a questioning tone into your voice by making it go up at the end.

Sporting events

Guided

The big match

1   Read this extract from *Sara y las goleadoras 5* by Laura Gallego.

> Mientras sus rivales celebraban el gol, Sara y sus amigas regresaron a sus posiciones con la cabeza baja, sin atreverse a mirar a las gradas,* desde donde las observaban los chicos.
>
> Sara miró el reloj: no llevaban ni diez minutos de partido y ya perdían por un gol. Pero lo peor no era eso; después de todo, un gol se podía remontar. No, lo peor de todo había sido aquella sensación de impotencia ante un equipo que era mucho mejor que el suyo.
>
> Angustiada, Sara volvió la vista hacia su entrenador, pero él le indicó con gestos que se calmara. Aún quedaba mucho partido por delante.

*gradas = terraces

Answer the following questions **in English.**

(a) What had the rival team done at the start of the extract?

.... **(1 mark)**

(b) Why didn't the girls want to look at the terraces?

.... **(1 mark)**

(c) What was the score ten minutes into the match?

.... **(1 mark)**

(d) Why did Sara feel powerless?

.... **(1 mark)**

(e) What did their trainer tell her to do by gesturing?

.... **(1 mark)**

Local sports events

LISTENING TRACK 83

Listen to the recording

2   Your Spanish friend is talking about sporting events near his home. What does he say?

Listen to the recording and complete the sentences by putting a cross [×] in the correct box for each question.

(i) The local football club …

☐	**A** provides employment for many.
☐	**B** is having building work done.
☐	**C** charges a fortune for merchandise.
☐	**D** invests money in local events.

(ii) The recent athletics championship …

☐	**A** was postponed due to bad weather.
☐	**B** took place last month.
☐	**C** was sold out.
☐	**D** inspired many local schools.

(iii) The swimming event …

☐	**A** caused huge traffic problems.
☐	**B** provided a great new facility.
☐	**C** was poorly attended.
☐	**D** created rows over the cost.

(3 marks)

Music events

A concert

1　Read these opinions on a forum from people who went to a recent concert.

Raúl	Una buena noche para mis amigos y yo. Ese guitarrista de la banda era fenomenal. Lástima que no tocaran más tiempo.
Lidia	¡Qué bien lo pasamos! Gracias a la banda por tocar sus viejas canciones además de las más recientes.
Iván	Si os digo la verdad, no lo pasé muy bien. Fui con mi amiga que quería ver el grupo pero ese tipo de música no es de mi gusto.
Celia	Fui al concierto sin conocer su música y ahora soy una de sus más fieles fans. Compré una camiseta al final del concierto y hoy descargué su álbum.

Who says what about the concert? Enter **Raúl**, **Lidia**, **Iván** or **Celia**.
You can use each person more than once.

(a)　.............................. only went to keep a friend company.　　**(1 mark)**

(b)　.............................. didn't know the band beforehand.　　**(1 mark)**

(c)　.............................. felt the band should have played longer.　　**(1 mark)**

(d)　.............................. was pleased with the range of songs played.　　**(1 mark)**

(e)　.............................. has bought some band merchandise.　　**(1 mark)**

(f)　.............................. didn't enjoy the type of music.　　**(1 mark)**

Taking part

LISTENING TRACK 84

Listen to the recording

2　Your Valencian friend Andrés is telling you about a musical event he is involved in.
What does he mention?

Listen to the recording and put a cross [×] in each one of the **three** correct boxes.

A	the cost of the tickets	☐
B	where the concert will be	☐
C	the type of music they will play	☐
D	what the concert is in aid of	☐
E	the starting time	☐
F	the date of the concert	☐
G	how many people are in the orchestra	☐

(3 marks)

> Remember that in this type of exercise you won't hear words like *fecha* (date) or *donde* (where), the English equivalent of which you see in the questions. Instead you will hear a day or month, giving a date, and a location or venue, indicating where the concert is.

Green issues

Campañas medioambientales

1 Lee este artículo sobre unas iniciativas verdes.

Campaña Planeta
Trabajamos con las especies amenazadas para protegerlas y para conseguir que tengan un futuro más seguro. Visitamos centros de enseñanza para hacer presentaciones sobre las causas de su desaparición.

Campaña Mundo
Nuestros científicos siguen buscando maneras de canalizar las fuerzas naturales del viento y del sol para reemplazar el uso tradicional de combustibles fósiles.

Campaña Tierra
Nuestro grupo trabaja sin cesar para proteger las zonas salvajes de nuestro planeta como selvas tropicales y bosques antiguos. Estas zonas son los pulmones de nuestra tierra.

Campaña Global
Nuestro equipo investiga fábricas y empresas que no cumplen con las leyes de seguridad y limpieza; y de esta forma contaminan los ríos, el aire y la tierra a su alrededor.

¿Qué campaña corresponde a cada frase? Escoge entre **Planeta**, **Mundo**, **Tierra** o **Global**. Puedes usar las palabras más de una vez.

> With questions all in Spanish, you will often need to look out for synonyms, and it is worthwhile learning some. For example: *planeta, mundo, tierra* (planet, world, earth); *viejo, antiguo, anciano* (old); *bosque, árboles, selva* (wood, trees, forest).

(a) Intentamos evitar que corten los árboles. .... **(1 mark)**

(b) Trabajamos para que las industrias no causen polución. .... **(1 mark)**

(c) Investigamos las fuentes de energía alternativas. .... **(1 mark)**

(d) Intentamos interesar a los estudiantes en nuestra causa. .... **(1 mark)**

(e) Obligamos a las compañías a seguir la legislación. .... **(1 mark)**

Climate change

2 You are in a geography class in your Spanish friend's school, listening to a talk about climate change. What issues are mentioned?

Listen to the recording and put a cross [×] in each one of the **three** correct boxes.

Listen to the recording

A	earthquakes	☐
B	heavy rains	☐
C	floods	☐
D	desertification	☐
E	hurricanes	☐
F	drought	☐
G	spread of disease	☐

(3 marks)

Environmental action

Guided

Supporting campaigns

1   Read these opinions on a school forum about which initiative the school should support.

José	Lo mejor sería intentar reducir la cantidad de electricidad que se usa en el colegio. Si apagamos las luces y los ordenadores al final del día, ahorraremos mucha.
Ana	En mi opinión, deberíamos hacer algo con la enorme cantidad de papel y cartón que tiramos a la basura. Estoy segura de que podríamos llevarlo a una empresa de reciclaje.
Miguel	Yo recomiendo un día sin coches para reducir la cantidad de gasolina usada y de gases emitidos. Hay muchos estudiantes que no necesitan usar el transporte para llegar.
Pilar	Deberíamos organizar un grupo para ayudar a limpiar zonas sucias del barrio. El río está muy contaminado con basura y los peces están en peligro.

Who says what about possible initiatives? Enter either **José**, **Ana**, **Miguel** or **Pilar**.
You can use each person more than once.

(a) .... recommends a day of walking or cycling to school.   **(1 mark)**

(b) .... wants to use the services of a recycling company.   **(1 mark)**

(c) .... is concerned about local wildlife.   **(1 mark)**

(d) .... suggests cleaning up polluted areas nearby.   **(1 mark)**

(e) .... would like to prioritise cleaner air.   **(1 mark)**

(f) .... is trying to save energy.   **(1 mark)**

> The topic of the environment is not as challenging as you might expect, because many of the words are very similar in both languages. Note this key vocabulary: *electricidad* – electricity, *energía* – energy, *contaminación* – contamination/pollution, *reciclar* – to recycle.

Sea pollution

2   Your Spanish friend is telling you about an initiative she has heard of.

Listen to the recording and answer the following questions **in English**.

Listen to the recording

(a) What are they trying to protect?

....   **(1 mark)**

(b) Which **two** groups of people are to blame for the pollution?

....   **(2 marks)**

(c) What are the **two** worst types of rubbish?

....   **(2 marks)**

(d) What is the fate of some fish?

....   **(1 mark)**

Had a go ☐ Nearly there ☐ Nailed it! ☐

Global issues

Guided

Poverty

1   Read this extract adapted from an Oxfam Intermón blog post.

> La pobreza es una epidemia que afecta a millones de personas en nuestro planeta. En el mundo, 1.400 millones de personas sufren pobreza extrema y casi 900 millones sufren hambre, no tienen acceso al agua potable y a otros servicios básicos como la salud y la educación.
>
> Hombres, mujeres, niños y niñas siguen sufriendo por hambre o malnutrición y viven en entornos donde la exclusión y la discriminación son protagonistas.
>
> El objetivo de muchas organizaciones como Oxfam Intermón es luchar contra la pobreza en el mundo. Sin embargo, para poder extirparla*, primero hay que entender cuáles son sus causas.

extirpar = get rid of

Answer the following questions **in English.**

(a) According to the blog post, how many people in the world suffer from hunger?

.... **(1 mark)**

(b) Which basic services do people affected by poverty lack?

.... **(1 mark)**

(c) What is the main goal of organisations like Oxfam Intermón?

.... **(1 mark)**

(d) What does the blog post say must be done first?

.... **(1 mark)**

Concerns about global issues

2   You are in a Spanish school, listening to a discussion about global issues.
    What issues concern these three students?

Listen to the recording and put a cross [×] in each one of the **three** correct boxes.

Listen to the recording

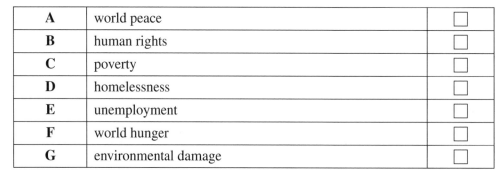

A	world peace	☐
B	human rights	☐
C	poverty	☐
D	homelessness	☐
E	unemployment	☐
F	world hunger	☐
G	environmental damage	☐

(3 marks)

Natural resources

Listen to the recording

Saving resources

1　You are listening to your Spanish friends discussing saving resources.

Listen to the recording and complete the sentences by putting a cross [×] in the correct box for each question.

(i)　The statistics show that …

☐	**A**	7% more people are reusing plastic bags.
☐	**B**	use of plastic bags has gone down 17%.
☐	**C**	most people still forget to bring a bag.
☐	**D**	the use of cloth bags went up 70%.

(ii)　Tomás and his family …

☐	**A**	turn leftover food into compost.
☐	**B**	tend to waste a lot of food.
☐	**C**	use up leftovers creatively.
☐	**D**	join in litter-picking campaigns.

(iii) Eva and her family …

☐	**A**	try to use public transport and not the car.
☐	**B**	grow a lot of their own food.
☐	**C**	sell organic produce on the market.
☐	**D**	use only natural pesticides.

(iv) Ricardo's father …

☐	**A**	has installed solar panels.
☐	**B**	is going to install solar panels.
☐	**C**	is currently installing solar panels.
☐	**D**	has decided against solar panels.

(v)　Ricardo's father is considering a generator …

☐	**A**	that uses less electricity.
☐	**B**	powered by the sun.
☐	**C**	fuelled by water from the river.
☐	**D**	driven by the wind.

(5 marks)

Listen to the recording

Natural resources

2　Mira la foto y prepara las respuestas a los siguientes puntos:

- la descripción de la foto
- las campañas medioambientales en tu instituto
- el reciclaje en tu casa
- ideas para evitar el malgasto del agua
- cómo reducir el uso de la electricidad en casa

Prepare your answers using the prompts. Then listen to the recording of the teacher's questions and answer in the pauses. There is a recording of one student's answers in the answer section to give you more ideas.

Had a go ☐ Nearly there ☐ Nailed it! ☐

Nouns and articles

Remember not all words ending in *a* are feminine or ending in *o* are masculine! There are exceptions.

1 Write the correct definite article *el, la, los, las*.

Example: la gente

(a) .... mesa

(b) .... fútbol

(c) .... patatas fritas

(d) .... dientes

(e) .... mano

(f) .... piso

(g) .... ciencias

(h) .... guisantes

(i) .... problema

(j) .... foto

2 Complete the sentences with either the definite article *el, la, los, las* or the indefinite article *un, una*. Remember to think about gender and whether it is singular or plural.

Example: En casa tengo un perro que es negro y blanco.

(a) En mi opinión, las zanahorias son más ricas que .... judías verdes.

(b) En mi casa hay .... cuarto de baño y tres dormitorios.

(c) No me gusta nada .... francés porque es complicado.

(d) Todos .... martes tengo club de ajedrez.

(e) En mi estuche hay .... regla y tres bolígrafos.

(f) Mi instituto es grande y hay .... campo de deportes.

(g) Me he roto .... pie y me duele mucho.

(h) .... domingo fuimos a una piscina al aire libre cerca de mi casa.

Often we use articles in English when in Spanish they are not needed, for example talking about jobs, and after *sin* and *con*. Sometimes we use articles in Spanish when we would not in English, for example talking generally (noun at the start of a sentence), expressing opinions, before the days of the week (*el lunes voy a …*).

3 Read the sentences and cross out any articles that have been used where they are not needed.

Example: No tengo ~~un~~ coche porque prefiero viajar en metro.

(a) Vivo en un cómodo bloque de pisos en las afueras.

(b) Mi padre es un dentista y mi madre es una enfermera.

(c) Hay muy pocos estudiantes en el instituto sin un móvil.

(d) Escribo con un lápiz en mi clase de matemáticas.

(e) En el futuro me gustaría ser una actriz.

(f) El deporte es muy importante para llevar una vida sana.

(g) Odio el dibujo porque no puedo dibujar bien.

(h) Se puede reservar dos habitaciones con una ducha.

Adjectives

> Most adjectives agree as follows:
>
> end in *–o*: *alto / alta / altos / altas*
>
> end in *–e*: add *–s* in the plural
>
> end in **consonant***: add *–es* in the plural
>
> *Nationalities also have a separate feminine singular form: *español**a***

1   Find the correct adjective from the list. Remember that as well as making sense, the adjective must agree with the noun.

Example: una periodista seria

(a)   una cama ....

(b)   dos gatos ....

(c)   un vestido ....

(d)   las películas son ....

(e)   el profesor es ....

(f)   las actrices son ....

(g)   la playa es ....

(h)   nuestros coches son ....

> cómoda
> baratos
> español
> interesantes
> preciosa
> rojo
> seria
> simpáticas
> traviesos

2   Choose the correct adjective.

Example: Vivo en un apartamento muy *pequeña /(pequeño)/ pequeños*.

(a)   Me alojé en un hotel *lujoso / lujosa / lujosos* de cuatro estrellas.

(b)   Me gusta llevar pantalones *cómodas / cómodos / cómodo*.

(c)   Creo que mi instituto es bastante *bueno / buen / buena*.

(d)   El paisaje era *impresionantes / impresionante / impresionan*.

(e)   La estación de tren está siempre *limpia / limpio / limpias*.

(f)   Me encantan las ciencias porque son muy *útiles / útil / utilizas*.

> Some adjectives have shortened forms which are positioned before the noun:
>
> *un coche bueno* ⟶ *un buen coche*

3   Write out these sentences with the correct adjective in the correct place.

Example:
Suelo comer fruta porque es sana y deliciosa. (mucho / mucha)
Suelo comer mucha fruta porque es sana y deliciosa.

(a)   En Inglaterra hay gente que habla muy bien griego. (poco / poca)

....

(b)   Lo mejor es que tiene un jardín. (bonito / bonita)

....

(c)   Estamos porque hace buen tiempo. (contento / contentas)

....

(d)   En el futuro habrá una estatua aquí en la plaza. (gran / grandes)

....

(e)   Nuestro apartamento está en el piso. (primera / primer)

....

Possessives and pronouns

1 Complete the table with the missing possessive adjectives.

English	Spanish singular	Spanish plural
my	mi	
your		tus
his / her / its		
our		nuestros / nuestras
your		
their	su	

2 Complete each sentence with the correct possessive adjective.

(a) My house is big.   .... casa es grande.

(b) His brother is the oldest.   .... hermano es el mayor.

(c) Their sons play tennis.   .... hijos juegan al tenis.

(d) My favourite films are comedies.   .... películas preferidas son las comedias.

(e) Its food is healthy.   .... comida es sana.

Possessive pronouns are like possessive adjectives but replace the noun they describe.
They must agree with the noun they replace!

In Spanish they are always accompanied by the definite article:

el mío / la mía / los míos / las mías = mine	el tuyo / la tuya = yours
el suyo / la suya = his / hers	el nuestro / la nuestra = ours

---

3 Complete these comparisons with the correct possessive pronoun.

Example: Nuestras toallas son más pequeñas que las tuyas. (yours)
             (Our towels are smaller than yours.)

(a) Tu perro es más inteligente que .... (mine)

(b) Mis gafas son menos feas que .... (his)

(c) Tu profe de historia es más callado que .... (ours)

(d) Su abrigo es más cómodo que .... (yours)

4 Rewrite the phrases to create one sentence using the relative pronoun *que*.

Example: Tengo un hermano. Se llama Diego ⟶ Tengo un hermano que se llama Diego.

(a) María tiene un gato. Es negro y pequeño.

....

(b) Vivimos en un pueblo. Está en el norte de Inglaterra.

....

(c) En la clase de literatura tengo que leer un libro. Es muy aburrido.

....

Comparisons

To form the comparative:	**más** + adjective + **que** = more … than
	menos + adjective + **que** = less … than
	tan + adjective + **como** = as … as

1 Read the English and then complete each Spanish sentence with the correct comparative adjective.

> **Example:** My sister is taller than my brother.
>
> Mi hermana es más alta que mi hermano.

(a) My mother is taller than my father.

Mi madre es .... mi padre.

(b) Mariela is less patient than Francisco.

Mariela es .... Francisco.

(c) This bus is slower than the train.

Este autobús es .... el tren.

(d) Fruit is as healthy as vegetables.

La fruta es .... las verduras.

(e) This shirt is as expensive as that jacket.

Esta camisa es .... aquella chaqueta.

Remember!
el / la mejor, los / las mejores = the best
el / la peor, los / las peores = the worst

2 Write out the correct superlative sentence.

> **Example:** Esta cafetería es la menos cara. (the least expensive)

(a) Mi profesor de inglés es .... (the best)

(b) Mis deberes de religión son .... (the worst)

(c) Mi mejor amiga es .... de la clase. (the smallest)

(d) Sus perros son .... (the most intelligent)

(e) Las noticias de Telecinco son .... (the least boring)

| *el / la* | + | *más* | + | adjective | = the most |
| *los / las* | | *menos* | | | = the least |

3 Translate these sentences **into Spanish**.

To translate words like 'incredibly' or 'extremely' don't forget to use the ending *-ísimo/a*.

> **Example:** My car is the cheapest. Mi coche es el más barato.

(a) My cousin is stronger than your uncle. ....

(b) Her mobile phone is incredibly small. ....

(c) The Spanish exam is extremely easy. ....

(d) Horror films are as exciting as action films. ....

(e) My school is the ugliest! ....

(f) Science is less boring than geography. ....

(g) Kylian Mbappé is the best. ....

Other adjectives

> Demonstrative adjectives are used to indicate which thing/person you are referring to ('this', 'those', etc.). There are three in Spanish: one for 'this'/'these', and two for 'that'/'those' (to distinguish between 'that' and 'that further away'). All forms need to agree with their noun in number and gender.

1   Complete the table with the correct demonstrative adjective.

English	Masculine singular	Feminine singular	Masculine plural	Feminine plural
this / these	este			
that / those		esa		
that (over there) / those (over there)			aquellos	

2   Translate into Spanish. (o/t = 'over there')

(a) these boots ....

(b) this t-shirt ....

(c) that girl (o/t) ....

(d) those bananas ....

(e) that mobile phone ....

(f) those magazines (o/t) ....

(g) this book ....

(h) that film ....

(i) that train (o/t) ....

(j) these hats ....

(k) those strawberries ....

(l) those boys (o/t) ....

3   Complete the sentences with the correct indefinite adjectives from the box below.

cada	todo / toda	algún / alguna	otro / otra
mismo / misma	todos / todas	algunos / algunas	otros / otras
mismos / mismas			

(a) Juega al baloncesto .... (every) día.

(b) Siempre da la .... (same) opinión.

(c) Conozco a .... (some) chicos que trabajan de peluqueros.

(d) Ayer, ... (all) los alumnos hicieron sus exámenes.

(e) Voy a hablar con Pablo porque él tiene .... (another) llave.

4   Fill in the gaps in the text using both demonstrative and indefinite adjectives. The text is translated for you below.

> El año pasado fui de vacaciones con mi familia. **(a)** .... los años vamos al sur de Inglaterra, pero este año fuimos a España. **(b)** .... de mis amigos han ido a España, pero esta fue mi primera vez. ¡Me gustó mucho! **(c)** .... los españoles que conocimos eran muy amables y **(d)** .... hablaban muy bien inglés. En España, a los jóvenes les gusta la **(e)** .... ropa que a los jóvenes ingleses y nos divierten los **(f)** .... pasatiempos. ¡Fue muy interesante!

> Last year I went on holiday with my family. Every year we go to the South of England but this year we went to Spain. Some of my friends have been to Spain but this was my first time. I liked it a lot! All the Spanish people we met were really nice and some spoke very good English. In Spain, the young people love the same clothes as English young people and we like the same hobbies. It was really interesting!

Pronouns

1 Complete the table with the correct subject pronouns in English or Spanish.

yo	
	you singular
	he
ella	

	we (masc.)
nosotras	
vosotros	
	you plural (fem.)
ellos	
	they (fem.)

A pronoun replaces a noun. An object pronoun has the action (shown by the verb) done to it. It can be direct or indirect.

She sent it to me. – **it** = direct object; **me** = indirect object

Direct object pronouns: *me*, *te*, *lo / la*, *nos*, *os*, *los / las*

Position of the object pronouns:

- Before a conjugated verb: *lo compro* (I buy it), *lo he comprado* (I have bought it)

- After a negative: *no lo compro* (I don't buy it)

- At the end of an infinitive or gerund (or before the verb): *voy a comprarlo / lo voy a comprar* (I am going to buy it), *estoy comprándolo / lo estoy comprando* (I am buying it)

---

2 Replace the noun with the correct object pronoun.

Example: Miguel ha perdido la maleta. → Miguel la ha perdido.

(a) Hemos perdido las llaves. ....

(b) Han perdido la moto. ....

(c) Teresa come el bocadillo. ....

(d) Compro el vestido. ....

(e) No bebo limonada. ....

(f) No lavo la ropa. ....

(g) Quiero escribir un correo electrónico. ....

(h) No quiero leer esa novela. ....

(i) Necesito la información ahora. ....

(j) Vamos a vender la casa. ....

> **Remember!**
> You only need to replace the noun. The verb will stay the same.

3 Translate these sentences, which use direct and indirect object pronouns, into English or Spanish.

Example: Le di mi cuaderno de matemáticas. → I gave him my Maths exercise book.

> Indirect object pronouns: *me, te, le, nos, os, les*

(a) Le voy a escribir esta tarde. ....

(b) Los visité ayer. ....

(c) Lo haré si tengo tiempo. ....

(d) Le di un regalo para su cumpleaños. ....

(e) ¿Las has visto? ....

(f) She came to visit me at home. ....

(g) They sent me the reservation. ....

(h) I am going to buy them online. ....

The present tense

To form the present tense, replace the infinitive ending with:

–ar verbs: *o, as, a, amos, áis, an*

–er verbs: *o, es, e, emos, éis, en*

–ir verbs: *o, es, e, imos, ís, en*

Tú is used for people you know and in the present tense the verb will always end in *s*.

Usted is the formal word for 'you' and the verb takes the same ending as *él* or *ella*, and therefore has no *s* at the end.

1   Write the verb in the correct person.

Example: escuchar (tú) ⟶ escuchas

(a) vivir (nosotros) ⟶ ....

(b) bailar (ellas) ⟶ ....

(c) vender (yo) ⟶ ....

(d) llevar (vosotros) ⟶ ....

(e) odiar (tú) ⟶ ....

(f) comer (él) ⟶ ....

(g) salir (nosotros) ⟶ ....

(h) escuchar (usted) ⟶ ....

2   Choose the correct verb for each sentence.

Example: En mi tiempo libre (practico) / *practican* deportes.

(a) Mis padres *comemos* / *comen* mucha carne.

(b) Mi hermana y yo *vive* / *vivimos* en un barrio precioso.

(c) ¿A qué hora *tienes* / *tienen* tu clase de natación?

(d) Nunca *habla* / *hablan* en francés porque son tímidos.

(e) Usted *debes* / *debe* firmar aquí.

(f) Nuestro amigo es paciente y nunca *grita* / *gritáis*.

(g) Normalmente *chateas* / *chateo* con mis amigos por Internet.

(h) A veces su profesor *lee* / *leen* en clase.

(i) ¿Usted qué *piensa* / *pensáis* del precio de la ropa?

(j) *Puedes* / *Podéis* comprar vuestros billetes aquí.

In the present tense, *er* and *ir* verbs are only different for the *nosotros* and *vosotros* parts of the verb and so there are fewer endings to learn!

3   Write the correct part of the verb in each sentence. Watch out for radical-changing verbs!

Example: Mis amigos estudian inglés, francés y español. (estudiar)

(a) Nos gusta la comida italiana y esta noche .... pizza. (cenar)

(b) Los mecánicos a veces .... al aire libre. (trabajar)

(c) Me levanto temprano y .... a las ocho y media. (desayunar)

(d) Limpia su dormitorio y luego .... la mesa. (poner)

(e) Nunca comemos caramelos, pero .... pasteles a menudo. (comprar)

(f) ¿Cuánto .... las cebollas? (costar)

(g) .... un teléfono móvil, pero no tengo dinero. (querer)

(h) Los niños .... mucho hoy en día. (pedir)

Reflexive verbs (present)

1 Write the correct reflexive pronoun next to each part of the verbs *afeitarse* and *vestirse*.

	afeito
te	afeitas
	afeita
	afeitamos
	afeitáis
se	afeitan

	visto
	vistes
	viste
	vestimos
	vestís
	visten

2 Complete the sentence with the correct reflexive pronoun.

Example: A veces mis amigos no se visten bien.

  (a)   Normalmente, los sábados, ... levanta a las nueve y media.

  (b)   Mis amigos no .... peinan, pero yo me peino siempre.

  (c)   ¿A qué hora .... despiertas los domingos?

  (d)   Los profesores .... quejan mucho de sus alumnos.

  (e)   Mis primos .... llaman John y Emma.

  (f)   .... levantamos temprano para ir de vacaciones.

  (g)   ¿ .... ducháis por la mañana o por la tarde?

  (h)   .... lavas y te vistes antes de ir al colegio.

3 Rewrite the story for Olivia. Change all the verbs in the 'I' form to the 'she' form. Don't forget to change the non-reflexive verbs too!

> Todos los días me levanto temprano para ir a trabajar. Trabajo en una tienda de ropa famosa. Primero me lavo los dientes y luego me ducho y me visto. Bajo las escaleras y desayuno cereales con fruta. Siempre me peino en la cocina. Después, me lavo la cara en el cuarto de baño que está abajo, al lado de la cocina. Me pongo la chaqueta y salgo a las ocho y media porque el autobús llega a las nueve menos cuarto. Vuelvo a casa a las siete de la tarde.

Todos los días Olivia se levanta

....

....

....

....

....

....

....

....

> **Remember!** Some verbs are regular but have an irregular ending in the first person singular.
> *Poner* is one of those verbs: *pongo, pones, pone*, etc. It can be reflexive when it means putting on clothes. Watch out for *salir*, too – the first person is *salgo*.

Irregular verbs (present)

1   Choose the correct verb for each sentence.

Example: Mis padres *decimos /* (*dicen*) que soy demasiado hablador.

(a) Mi hermano *conduce / conduces* demasiado rápido pero yo *conduzco / conducen* bien.

(b) Si Pablo *das / da* dinero a la causa, yo te *damos / doy* una contribución también.

(c) Cuando mi padre *oigo / oye* mi música, en seguida *salgo / sale* de la habitación.

(d) Si *haces / hace* buen tiempo, yo no *coge / cojo* el autobús.

(e) Yolanda, cuando tú y Marcos *vienes / venís* a casa, siempre *traen / traéis* regalos.

2   Complete the sentences with the correct form of the verb.

Example: A las ocho yo salgo (salir) de casa.

(a) Sube el volumen, Carlos no .... (oír) muy bien.

(b) Nunca voy a Francia y, por eso, no .... (conocer) París.

(c) Nuestros primos .... (venir) a cenar esta noche.

(d) Cuando voy a la ciudad siempre .... (coger) el tren.

(e) Cada año, mi familia y yo .... (ir) de vacaciones a España.

(f) Mis amigos han decidido sus asignaturas pero yo no .... (saber) qué hacer.

(g) Marta, ¿................................ (tener) tu móvil en tu bolso?

(h) Si hace frío en casa, simplemente me .... (poner) un jersey.

(i) Es el cumpleaños de Elena así que yo .... (traer) un pastel.

(j) Mis profesores .... (decir) que voy a sacar buenas notas.

3   Translate these sentences **into Spanish**.

(a) I go to Spain. ....

(b) He has two sisters. ....

(c) I hear music. ....

(d) She tells lies. ....

(e) We catch the bus. ....

(f) They do their homework. ....

(g) You (tú) go out on Saturdays. ....

(h) I give classes. ....

(i) He brings bread. ....

(j) I set the table. ....

Vocabulary
a lie = *una mentira*
to set the table = *poner la mesa*

Had a go ☐ **Nearly there** ☐ **Nailed it!** ☐

Ser and *estar*

> *ser:* use for permanent things (e.g. nationality, occupation, colour, size, personality)
>
> *estar*: use for temporary things (e.g. illness, appearance, feelings) and location

1 Write the correct form of the verb *ser* or *estar*.

Example: Somos ingleses y vivimos en Londres. (ser – nosotros)

    (a) ¿Dónde .... el banco? (estar)

    (b) Mis abuelas .... muy generosas. (ser)

    (c) .... de Madrid, pero trabajo en Barcelona. (ser – yo)

    (d) El vestido .... verde con flores blancas. (ser)

    (e) .... las cuatro y media de la tarde. (ser)

    (f) El armario .... enfrente de la puerta. (estar)

    (g) .... muy tristes hoy porque las vacaciones han terminado. (estar – vosotros)

    (h) .... listos para el examen de teatro. (estar – nosotros)

2 Now translate the sentences from exercise 1 into English. In brackets, write down the reason why the verb is *ser* or *estar*.

Example: We are English and we live in London. ('ser' for nationalities)

    (a) ....

    (b) ....

    (c) ....

    (d) ....

    (e) ....

    (f) ....

    (g) ....

    (h) ....

3 Tick the phrases which use the correct verb 'to be'. Correct those which are wrong.

Example: Estoy en Francia de vacaciones. ✓

           La plaza es a mano izquierda. ✗ La plaza está a mano izquierda.

    (a) Somos británicos y hablamos inglés.

    ....

    (b) Mi amigo está inteligente y tiene el pelo negro.

    ....

    (c) Me duele la cabeza y soy enfermo.

    ....

    (d) Mi perro ha muerto y estoy muy triste.

    ....

    (e) Su primo es italiano y trabaja como diseñador.

    ....

    (f) Mi madre está médica y mi padre está ingeniero.

    ....

    (g) Creo que hoy, después de ir a la peluquería, estoy guapo.

    ....

    (h) Mi casa está bastante pequeña, tiene solo un dormitorio.

    ....

The gerund

> Gerunds are –ing words (playing, singing, etc.). To form them replace the infinitive endings as follows:
> *hablar* – *hablando*, *comer* – *comiendo*, *vivir* – *viviendo*.
>
> Remember! Some verbs have irregular gerunds:
>
> *caer* → *cayendo*   *oír* → *oyendo*   *poder* → *pudiendo*
>
> Some radical-changing *ir* verbs also change their stem in the gerund:
>
> *pedir* → *pidiendo*   *dormir* → *durmiendo*

1 Change the following infinitives into the gerund, and write their meanings in English.

Example: beber → bebiendo - drinking

(a) comer → ....

(b) saltar → ....

(c) correr → ....

(d) tomar → ....

(e) dormir → ....

(f) asistir → ....

(g) escribir → ....

(h) escuchar → ....

(i) aprender → ....

(j) poder → ....

2 What are these people doing? Write sentences using the words from the box.

comer pizza	~~nadar en la piscina~~	tocar la guitarra
hablar con amigos	escuchar música	ver una película
navegar por Internet	escribir una postal	montar en bicicleta

Example: (he) Está nadando en la piscina.

(a) (she) ....
....

(b) (I) ....
....

(c) (they) ....
....

(d) (we) ....
....

(e) (you singular) ....
....

> The imperfect continuous is formed using the imperfect tense of ***estar*** + the gerund:
>
> *estaba comiendo* – I was eating
>
> ***estar*** in the imperfect tense: *estaba, estabas, estaba, estábamos, estabais, estaban*

3 Translate the first part of the sentences into Spanish.

Example: (I was fishing) Estaba pescando cuando me caí al agua.

(a) (she was sailing) .... cuando llegó la tormenta.

(b) (they were eating) .... cuando su madre les llamó.

(c) (we were sunbathing) .... cuando empezó a llover.

(d) (you were singing) .... cuando salió el tren.

(e) (we were watching TV) .... cuando nuestro hermanastro volvió a casa.

(f) (I was playing video games) .... cuando llamó.

(g) (you all were listening to the teacher) .... cuando entró el perro.

(h) (he was swimming in the sea) .... cuando apareció el tiburón.

The preterite tense

The preterite tense is used to describe completed actions in the past. Replace the infinitive ending with:

–ar verbs: *é, aste, ó, amos, asteis, aron*

–er and *–ir* verbs: *í, iste, ió, imos, isteis, ieron*

Remember! There are lots of irregular verbs in the preterite.

Some have irregular spellings in the first person: *saqué, toqué, crucé, empecé, llegué, jugué*

The most common irregular verbs are: *ir, ser, hacer, dar, decir, estar* and *tener.*

1   Write the verb in the correct form of the preterite tense.

   Example: comer (tú) ⟶ *comiste*

   (a) sacar (ellos) ⟶ ....   (f) ir (usted) ⟶ ....
   (b) volver (nosotros) ⟶ ....   (g) dar (yo) ⟶ ....
   (c) comprar (él) ⟶ ....   (h) tener (nosotros) ⟶ ....
   (d) llegar (tú) ⟶ ....   (i) visitar (ellas) ⟶ ....
   (e) trabajar (vosotros) ⟶ ....   (j) beber (él) ⟶ ....

2   Complete the sentences with the verb in the correct form of the preterite. All these sentences use irregular verbs.

   (a) La semana pasada .... (ir) a casa de mis amigos.
   (b) Mi novio y yo no .... (tener) tiempo para visitar el museo.
   (c) Sus padres nos .... (dar) unos regalos bonitos.
   (d) Conchita .... (ir) a la playa con su hermano.
   (e) El camarero me .... (dar) un café y yo .... (pagar) en seguida.
   (f) El invierno pasado mis padres .... (ir) de vacaciones solos.
   (g) 'No es verdad', ... (decir) el niño.
   (h) El concierto .... (ser) impresionante. Me gustó mucho.
   (i) .... (hacer) mis deberes antes de jugar al fútbol.
   (j) Anoche .... (tener) que poner y quitar la mesa y luego salí con mis amigos.

3   Read the text in the present tense and rewrite the text, changing all the verbs in bold into the preterite.

   Voy al cine con mis amigos y **vemos** una película de acción. Después **comemos** en un restaurante italiano. **Como** una pizza con jamón y queso, y mi amiga Lola **come** pollo con pasta. **Bebemos** zumo de manzana y mi amigo Tom **come** una tarta de chocolate pero yo no **como** postre. Después del restaurante **voy** en tren a casa de mi prima. El viaje **es** largo y aburrido. **Vuelvo** a casa y **me acuesto** a las once de la noche.

   Fui al cine con mis amigos

   ....
   ....
   ....
   ....
   ....
   ....
   ....

The imperfect tense

Remember! The imperfect is used:
- to describe repeated actions in the past
- when you would say 'used to' in English
- to describe background details.

Replace the infinitive ending with:

–ar verbs: *aba, abas, aba, ábamos, abais, aban*

–er and *–ir* verbs: *ía, ías, ía, íamos, íais, ían*

1 Tick the sentences which contain imperfect verbs and underline the verbs.

Example: Antes mi colegio <u>era</u> más pequeño. ✓

(a) El miércoles fuimos a la piscina y nadamos durante una hora y media.

(b) De pequeños nadábamos en el mar todas las semanas.

(c) Había mucha gente en el museo y las estatuas eran preciosas.

(d) Mi padre nos preparó una cena vegetariana.

(e) Cuando eran más jóvenes, no comían ni tomate ni lechuga.

(f) Gabriela llegó a Madrid en tren para empezar su nuevo trabajo.

(g) Ayer nos encontramos en la cafetería y hablamos toda la tarde.

(h) Me ponía nervioso cada vez que hacía una prueba de vocabulario.

(i) Lo pasé genial porque hizo sol y no llovió.

(j) Nevaba todos los días y hacía un frío horrible.

2 Translate the sentences from exercise 1 into English. Explain your choice of tense in brackets. Write your answers on a separate piece of paper.

Example: My school used to be smaller. (imperfect for 'used to')

3 Complete the sentences with the correct verb in the past tense. It could be either the preterite or the imperfect.

Example: El sábado fuimos a la discoteca a bailar y a divertirnos. (ir)

(a) Cuando mi hermana .... tres años empezó a tocar el piano. (tener)

(b) Mi familia .... en el campo, pero ahora tiene un piso en Londres. (vivir)

(c) .... lloviendo cuando llegamos al camping. (estar)

(d) La semana pasada .... la aspiradora y planché la ropa. (pasar)

(e) Todos los días .... en el jardín y plantaban muchas rosas. (trabajar)

(f) Hizo compras por Internet y .... mucho dinero. (gastar)

(g) Siempre .... fruta y bebíamos mucha agua para estar en forma. (comer)

(h) Una vez .... al tenis con mi profesor de inglés, pero no gané. (jugar)

The future tense

The **immediate future** tense is used to say what's going to happen. It is formed using the present tense of *ir* + *a* + an infinitive: *Voy a salir a las dos*. I'm going to go out at 2.

Present tense of *ir*: *voy, vas, va, vamos, vais, van*

1 Complete the sentences with the missing parts of the immediate future tense.

Example: I am going to buy a dress. Voy a comprar un vestido.

(a) We are going to play basketball. Vamos a .... al baloncesto.

(b) He is going to lay the table. .... a poner la mesa.

(c) They are going to eat lamb chops. Van .... comer chuletas de cordero.

(d) I am not going to cry. No .... a llorar.

(e) Are you going to watch the film? ¿ .... a ver la película?

(f) You (all) are going to listen and repeat. .... a escuchar y a repetir.

(g) My mother is going to catch the bus. Mi madre .... a coger el autobús.

(h) My friends are going to go to Scotland. Mis amigos van a .... a Escocia.

(i) We are not going to work Saturdays. No .... a trabajar los sábados.

(j) I am going to go out with my girlfriend. .... a salir con mi novia.

The **future tense** is used to talk about what you will do or what will happen in the future. The future tense is formed by adding these endings onto the infinitive:

-é, -ás, -á, -emos, -éis, -án

Don't forget the accents!

Remember there are some irregular future verbs: *saldré, diré, tendré, haré, podré, pondré, querré, sabré, vendré.*

2 Write the Spanish for these future sentences. Remember to use the future tense when describing what will happen.

Example: I will buy a dress. Compraré un vestido.

(a) We are going to watch the film. ....

(b) I will not work on Mondays. ....

(c) They are going to catch the underground. ....

(d) He will go to England. ....

(e) They are going to play with my brother. ....

(f) You will go to Spain. ....

3 Complete the text with the correct verbs in the immediate future tense.

seguir	aprender	trabajar	tener	ir	tomar	ser	vivir	ir

El año que viene mi amiga **(a)** .... a la universidad a estudiar Biología. Yo no

(b) .... a la universidad porque me **(c)** .... un año sabático. Quiero

trabajar como voluntaria, pero **(d)** .... que vivir con mis padres para ahorrar dinero.

(e) .... como voluntaria para una asociación benéfica que cuida a los sin techo.

(f) .... muy interesante, y me imagino que **(g)** .... mucho también.

Mi hermana **(h)** .... estudiando en el cole y mi hermano **(i)** .... en

el extranjero.

The conditional tense

> The conditional is used to describe what you would do or what would happen in the future. To form the conditional, add the following endings to the infinitive:
>
> *ía, ías, ía, íamos, íais, ían*
>
> There are a few verbs with irregular stems and these are the same as in the future tense.

1   Change these future verbs into the conditional. Write the English for each.

Example: haré ⟶ haría – I would do

(a) compraremos ⟶ ....

(b) saldrán ⟶ ....

(c) trabajaréis ⟶ ....

(d) estará ⟶ ....

(e) jugarás ⟶ ....

(f) vendremos ⟶ ....

(g) podrás ⟶ ....

(h) habrá ⟶ ....

2   In an ideal world what would happen next year? Create sentences using the conditional.

Example: Mi madre *compraría* un perro.

(a) Mi profesor .... de vacaciones.

(b) Nuestros primos .... el sol en la playa.

(c) El jefe no .... todos los días.

(d) Mis amigos y yo .... la lotería.

(e) No .... contaminación atmosférica.

(f) Más gente .... el transporte público.

(g) Las empresas no .... el agua.

(h) Los gobiernos .... contra la pobreza mundial.

(i) Mi equipo de fútbol .... la liga nacional.

(j) Mi hermano y yo no .... el dormitorio.

malgastar
(= to waste)
ir
ganar
haber
compartir
~~comprar~~
trabajar
usar
luchar
tomar
ganar

3   Give advice using the conditional of *deber* or *poder* to help these people.

Example: Tengo dolor de cabeza. –
Deberías / Podrías tomar una aspirina.

(a) No puedo dormir.

....

(b) Como demasiado chocolate.

....

(c) No tengo energía.

....

(d) Estoy enfermo. ....

(e) Estoy cansado todo el tiempo. ....

(f) Me duelen las muelas. ....

(g) Quiero reducir la contaminación. ....

(h) Debo gastar menos dinero. ....

tomar una aspirina
acostarte temprano
comer más frutas y verduras
comprar ropa de segunda mano
consumir menos energía
ir al médico
ir al dentista
hacer más ejercicio
evitar el estrés

Perfect and pluperfect

The perfect tense is used to talk about what someone **has done** or what **has happened**; the pluperfect is used to talk about what someone **had done** or what **had happened**.

Perfect: present tense of **haber** + a past participle.

Pluperfect: imperfect tense of **haber** + a past participle.

To form the past participle replace the infinitive ending with:
–ar verbs: **ado**
–er and **–ir** verbs: **ido**

1   Complete the table with the correct parts of the verb *haber*.

	Perfect tense (I have … etc.)	Pluperfect tense (I had … etc.)	+ past participles (spoken, eaten, lived, etc.)
yo	he		hablado comido vivido
tú			
él / ella / usted		había	
nosotros / nosotras	hemos		
vosotros /vosotras			
ellos / ellas / ustedes		habían	

Irregular past participles!

abrir ⟶ abierto   escribir ⟶ escrito   poner ⟶ puesto   ver ⟶ visto
decir ⟶ dicho   hacer ⟶ hecho   romper ⟶ roto   volver ⟶ vuelto

2   Translate these phrases into English or Spanish. The box above will help you.

Example: He hablado con él. I have spoken to him.

(a) Hemos perdido el coche. ....

(b) ¿Has estudiado español? ....

(c) Han comprado un ordenador portátil. ....

(d) He hecho mis deberes. ....

(e) Hemos visto un documental muy informativo. ....

(f) I have broken my arm. ....

(g) They have lost their suitcase. ....

(h) We have eaten lots of sweets. ....

(i) Have you visited the museum today? ....

(j) The air stewards have opened the doors. ....

3   Change the verbs into the pluperfect to tell the story.

Esta mañana ha sido horrible. **(a)** Había desayunado (desayunar) cuando sonó mi móvil.
Mi amiga **(b)** .... (perder) el bolso en el polideportivo y no tenía dinero
suficiente para pagar la entrada. Ella **(c)** .... (nadar) en la piscina y también
(d) .... (hacer) una clase de aerobic. Así que fui al polideportivo para ayudar
a mi amiga, pero yo me **(e)** .... (dejar) la bici en el cole y por eso cogí el
autobús. El viaje duró mucho y cuando llegué, mi amiga ya **(f)** .... (encontrar)
su bolso y su dinero. ¡Qué desastre!

Giving instructions

To give commands:

– to one person (**tú**): use the 'you' singular form of the present tense, minus the final *s*:
¡Escucha! Listen!   *¡Abre!* Open!

– to more than one person (**vosotros**): change the final *r* of the infinitive to *d*:
¡Escuchad! Listen!   *¡Abrid!* Open!

Irregular *tú* commands include:

	decir	hacer	ir	oír	poner	salir	tener	venir
tú	di	haz	ve	oye	pon	sal	ten	ven
English	say	make/do	go	hear	put	leave	have	come

1   Change the following infinitives into familiar singular commands (*tú*). Be careful, some are irregular in command form.

Example: Hablar más ⟶ Habla más.

(a) Doblar a la derecha ⟶ ....

(b) Cruzar la plaza ⟶ ....

(c) Pasar el puente ⟶ ....

(d) Tener cuidado ⟶ ....

(e) Venir aquí ⟶ ....

(f) Cantar más bajo ⟶ ....

(g) Leer en voz alta ⟶ ....

(h) Escuchar bien ⟶ ....

(i) Poner la mesa ⟶ ....

(j) Hacer este ejercicio ⟶ ....

2   Now change the above commands into familiar plural ones (*vosotros*). Remember, to form the *vosotros* commands, you change the *r* of the infinitive to *d*.

Example: Habla más. ⟶ Hablad más.

(a) ....

(b) ....

(c) ....

(d) ....

(e) ....

(f) ....

(g) ....

(h) ....

(i) ....

(j) ....

3   Translate these sentences **into Spanish**, using either *tú* or *vosotros* commands.

Example: Listen now! (vosotros) ⟶ ¡Escuchad ahora!

(a) Download the music! (tú) ....

(b) Turn left! (vosotros) ....

(c) Clear the table! (tú) ....

(d) Make the bed! (tú) ....

(e) Do the hoovering! (vosotros) ....

The present subjunctive

The subjunctive is used in a range of contexts, for example:

– to express doubt or uncertainty: *No creo que venga*. I don't think he's coming.

– to express a wish with **querer que**: *Quiero que te calles*. I wish you'd be quiet.

– after **cuando** with the future: *Cuando llegue, le contestaré*. When he arrives, I'll ask him.

– after **ojalá**: *Ojalá haga sol*. Let's hope it's sunny.

– to deny that information is true: *No es verdad que sea tímida*. It's not true that she's shy.

– to give negative *tú* commands: *¡No vayas!* Don't go!

The subjunctive is formed by replacing the **–o** ending of the present tense 'I' form with:

–ar verbs: *e, es, e, emos, éis, en*

–er and **–ir** verbs: *a, as, a, amos, áis, an*

Therefore verbs which are irregular in the first person in the present are irregular in the present subjunctive.

ir and *ser* have irregular stems: *vay– (ir)* and *se– (ser)*. The endings are the same.

1 Change these verbs from the present indicative into the present subjunctive.

Example: tenemos ⟶ tengamos

   (a) habla ⟶ ....   (f) sale ⟶ ....

   (b) comen ⟶ ....   (g) puede ⟶ ....

   (c) voy ⟶ ....   (h) hacen ⟶ ....

   (d) vives ⟶ ....   (i) encuentro ⟶ ....

   (e) trabajáis ⟶ ....   (j) somos ⟶ ....

2 Use the present subjunctive to make these positive *tú* and *vosotros* commands into negative ones.

Example: Habla con él. ⟶ No hables con él.

   (a) Come este pastel. ⟶ ....

   (b) Compra aquel vestido. ⟶ ....

   (c) Toma esa calle. ⟶ ....

   (d) Bebe un vaso de zumo de naranja. ⟶ ....

   (e) Ve esta película romántica. ⟶ ....

   (f) Firmad aquí. ⟶ ....

   (g) Rellenad este formulario. ⟶ ....

   (h) Abrid las ventanas. ⟶ ....

3 Complete these sentences with the verb in the correct form of the present subjunctive.

Example: Ojalá mi amiga venga (venir) a visitarme.

   (a) No creo que los jóvenes .... (escribir) a mano.

   (b) No es cierto que .... (hacer) siempre calor en el sur.

   (c) Ojalá nosotros .... (tener) suerte con los exámenes.

   (d) No creo que mis profesores .... (ser) estrictos.

   (e) Cuando .... (ir) a España, compraré un sombrero.

   (f) Dudo que los adolescentes .... (comprar) esos libros.

Negatives

To make a sentence negative, use *no* in front of the whole verb:
No me gusta la música jazz. — I don't like jazz music.
No vamos a visitar el palacio. — We are not going to visit the palace.

1 Write these sentences in the negative.

Example: Tengo clase hoy a las diez. → No tengo clase hoy a las diez.

(a) Estudio geografía. → ....

(b) Vamos a las afueras. → ....

(c) Ricardo compró una moto nueva. → ....

(d) Sus padres vieron la tele. → ....

(e) Voy a ir a Francia la semana que viene. → ....

2 Match the English and Spanish.

1	no … ni … ni …	**A**	never
2	no … nada	**B**	not … either
3	no … tampoco	**C**	no/not any
4	no … nadie	**D**	nothing/not anything
5	no … jamás	**E**	not … (either) … or …
6	no … nunca	**F**	never
7	no … ningún/ninguna	**G**	no one

3 Rewrite the sentence with the negative words.

Example: Mateo habla mucho de sus vacaciones. (no, nunca)
　　　　　Mateo no habla nunca de sus vacaciones.

Note that *ninguno* must agree with the noun it precedes: *ninguna ropa* (no clothes)

(a) Mis profesores enseñan cómo repasar. (no, nunca) ....

(b) En mi casa tuvimos una sala de juegos. (no, jamás) ....

(c) Me he quemado los brazos. (no, nunca) ....

(d) Aquí tengo vestidos, faldas y camisetas. (no, ni, ni, ni) ....

(e) Vas a comprar un coche. (no, ningún) ....

(f) Mis padres escuchan. (no, a nadie) ....

4 Translate the sentences **into Spanish**. Be careful with the word order.

Example: He never plays football when it rains.
　　　　　Nunca juega al fútbol cuando llueve. / No juega nunca al fútbol cuando llueve.

(a) In the afternoon we never drink coffee. ....

(b) I don't iron, cook or clean. ....

(c) They do not speak any languages. ....

(d) We can't talk to anybody during the exam. ....

....

(e) I will never smoke because it is a waste of money. ....

....

Special verbs

> A few verbs like *gustar* are generally used in the 3rd person with a pronoun:
> *Me gusta bailar.* I like dancing.
>
> If the thing that is liked is plural, you use *me gustan*: *Me gustan los perros.* I like dogs.
> *encantar*, *doler*, *apetecer* and *faltar* behave in the same way:
> *Le duele la cabeza.* His head hurts.
> *Hacen falta dos vasos.* Two glasses are needed.
> *¿Te apetece salir a comer?* Do you fancy going out to eat?

1 Complete the table with the correct pronouns.

me	gusta (sing)	I like
		you like
	gustan (plu)	he / she / it likes

	gusta (sing)	we like
		you (all) like
	gustan (plu)	they like

2 Tick the sentences which use the impersonal verb correctly. Correct the other sentences.

> Remember! If the impersonal verb is followed by an infinitive, the singular form is always used:
> *Les **gusta** tocar la guitarra.* = They like to play the guitar.
> When the subject is a noun or a proper noun, you need to use *a*:
> *A Paz le gusta correr.* = Paz likes to run.

Example: Me gusta mucho los idiomas y por eso quiero viajar más. ✗

　　　　　Me gustan mucho los idiomas y por eso quiero viajar más.

(a) A Pilar y a Pablo les interesan los ordenadores y la informática.

....

(b) Nos apetecen ir al cine mañana.

....

(c) Es verdad que le duelen mucho los ojos.

....

(d) No nos gustan la contaminación atmosférica.

....

(e) ¿Te hace falta unas toallas?

....

3 Unjumble the words to make sentences using an impersonal verb.

Example: gustan / las / me / zanahorias / mucho Me gustan mucho las zanahorias.

(a) falta / abrigo / nos / un / hace ....

(b) os / caballos / encantan / los / negros ....

(c) María / le / aquellos / zapatos / a / gustan ....

(d) quedan / veinte / te / euros / regalo / comprar / para / el

....

(e) todo / me / el / la / cabeza / tiempo / duele

....

(f) encantan / rascacielos / porque / les / son / modernos / los

....

Por and *para*

Remember that *por* and *para* don't just mean 'for'. They can be translated in various ways depending on the sentence. For example: in, in order to, per, instead of, etc.

1 Translate these sentences, which use *para*, **into English**.

(a) Para mi cumpleaños quiero un móvil nuevo.

....

(b) Mi amiga trabaja para un arquitecto.

....

(c) Las aplicaciones para iPhone son increíbles.

....

(d) Como muchas verduras y pescado para estar en forma.

....

(e) Necesitas la llave para entrar en casa.

....

(f) Fumar es muy malo para la salud.

....

(g) Van a organizar una fiesta para celebrar el fin de curso.

....

(h) Para mí, los deportes son siempre divertidos.

....

2 Rewrite the sentences with the word *por* in the correct place.

Example: Muchas gracias los pantalones. Muchas gracias por los pantalones.

(a) El coche rojo pasó las calles antiguas.

....

(b) Normalmente la mañana me gusta desayunar cereales y fruta.

....

(c) Mandé la reserva correo electrónico.

....

(d) Me gustaría cambiar este jersey otro.

....

(e) En la tienda ganamos diez euros hora.

....

(f) Había mucha basura todas partes.

....

3 Complete the sentence with either *por* or *para*.

Example: Por la tarde prefiero descansar.

(a) .... mantener la piel sana, lo más importante es beber mucha agua.

(b) Mis amigas compraron unas flores .... la profesora.

(c) Tengo que cambiar este diccionario .... otro.

(d) Hemos reservado una habitación .... tres noches.

(e) Los alumnos tienen que completar los ejercicios .... el lunes.

Questions and exclamations

Don't forget that Spanish question words have accents. Questions and exclamations have an inverted question mark (¿) or exclamation mark (¡) at the beginning.

1 Use the question words in the box to complete the table below.

| ¿~~Qué?~~ | ¿Cuánto? | ¿Dónde? | ¿Cuándo? | ¿Cuáles? |
| ¿Adónde? | ¿Por qué? | ¿Cuántos? | ¿Cómo? | ¿~~Cuál?~~ |

1	Why?	
2	What?	¿Qué?
3	When?	
4	How?	
5	Where?	
6	Where to?	
7	Which?	¿Cuál?
8	Which ones?	
9	How much?	
10	How many?	

2 Match the Spanish and the English for these exclamations. Write the correct letters in the grid.

1 ¡Qué lástima!	**A** What a problem!
2 ¡Qué va!	**B** How strange!
3 ¡Qué rollo!	**C** How cool!
4 ¡Qué difícil!	**D** How terrible!
5 ¡Qué problema!	**E** No way!
6 ¡Qué guay!	**F** What a shame!
7 ¡Qué bien!	**G** How boring!
8 ¡Qué raro!	**H** How embarrassing!
9 ¡Qué vergüenza!	**I** How good!
10 ¡Qué horror!	**J** How difficult!

1	2	3	4	5	6	7	8	9	10
F									

3 Complete the question or exclamation with the appropriate word or phrase.

| rollo | guay | cómo | cuánto | ~~dónde~~ | horror |

Example: ¿De dónde son ustedes?

(a) Me he roto la pierna. ¡Qué .... !

(b) ¿ .... cuesta el jamón serrano?

(c) ¿ .... es tu casa, Ramona?

(d) Vamos a ir de vacaciones.

   ¡Qué .... !

(e) El viaje en autocar va a durar ocho horas.

   ¡Qué .... !

Connectives and adverbs

Not all adverbs end in *–mente*:

bien – well   *siempre* – always   *bastante* – enough   *poco* – a little
mal – badly   *demasiado* – too   *a menudo* – frequently / often

1   Turn these adjectives into adverbs. Remember to make them feminine first!

     Example: fácil ⟶ fácilmente

     (a) rápido ⟶ ....

     (b) difícil ⟶ ....

     (c) lento ⟶ ....

     (d) alegre ⟶ ....

     (e) tranquilo ⟶ ....

2   Match the connectives correctly. Write the correct letters in the grid.

1 además de	**A** but
2 y / e	**B** therefore
3 pero	**C** although
4 sin embargo	**D** also
5 también	**E** and
6 por eso / por lo tanto	**F** if
7 porque	**G** because
8 ya que	**H** then
9 si	**I** or
10 o / u	**J** since
11 aunque	**K** however
12 entonces	**L** as well as

1	2	3	4	5	6	7	8	9	10	11	12
L											

3   Rewrite sentences a–e with the correct adverb. Complete sentences f–h with the correct connective.

     Example: Los alumnos juegan al rugby. (well) *Los alumnos juegan bien al rugby.*

     (a) Sus padres cantan en la iglesia. (badly)

     ....

     (b) No hablo porque soy tímido. (much)

     ....

     (c) El tren pasa por el túnel. (quickly)

     ....

     (d) Los pendientes son caros. (too)

     ....

     (e) Comemos huevos por la mañana. (frequently)

     ....

     (f) Vamos a ir a la piscina .... hace buen tiempo.

     (g) Odio mi instituto .... hay acoso escolar.

     (h) El piso es muy moderno, ... no tiene lavaplatos.

Remember! Adverbs can go before or after the verb they relate to:
Siempre como carne. / Como siempre carne.

Numbers

1 Write the number.

Example: trece 13

(a) veinte ....

(b) cuarenta y ocho ....

(c) nueve ....

(d) cien ....

(e) catorce ....

(f) mil ....

(g) trescientos ....

(h) cincuenta y siete ....

(i) veintitrés ....

(j) quince ....

(k) diecinueve ....

(l) quinientos ....

(m) un millón ....

(n) novecientos ....

(o) ochenta y ocho ....

(p) setenta y seis ....

(q) sesenta y siete ....

(r) diez ....

(s) cero ....

(t) veintinueve ....

> Ordinal numbers (*primero*, *segundo*, *tercero*, etc.) are not used for dates, except for *primero* which can be used. Both of these are correct:
>
> *el uno de diciembre*
>
> *el primero de diciembre*

2 Write these dates and years **in Spanish**.

Example: 4 May el cuatro de mayo

(a) 1999 ....

(b) 10 October ....

(c) 1 January ....

(d) 3 March ....

(e) 2013 ....

(f) 16 November ....

(g) 30 May ....

(h) 1968 ....

(i) 2002 ....

(j) 21 April ....

> To give the time, use *son las* + the number for the hour, except for 'one o'clock', which is *Es la una*.
> *Son las ocho.* It's eight o'clock.
> For times **past** the hour, add *y cinco*, *y diez* etc.: *Son las nueve y veinte.*
> For times **to** the hour, add *menos veinte*, *menos diez* etc.: *Son las tres menos diez.*
> a quarter past = *y cuarto*
> a quarter to = *menos cuarto*
> half past = *y media*

3 Write these times **in Spanish**.

Example: It's 5.25. Son las cinco y veinticinco

(a) It's 7.15 ....

(b) It's 1.25 ....

(c) It's 8.35. ....

(d) It's 11.10. ....

(e) It's 3.45. ....

(f) It's 9.50. ....

(g) It's 5.30. ....

(h) It's 12.00. ....

Test: Listening 1

Food and drink

Listen to the recording

1 Sergio is talking about what he usually eats.

What does he say?

Listen to the recording and answer the questions **in English**.

(a) What does he have at break? .... **(1 mark)**

(b) What is his favourite meal at lunch? .... **(1 mark)**

(c) What do they often have as a main course in the evening?

.... **(1 mark)**

Holidays

Listen to the recording

2 Your Spanish exchange partner, Verónica, is telling you about her trip to México.

What holiday highlights does she mention?

Listen to the recording and put a cross [×] in each one of the **three** correct boxes.

A	watching a dance show	☐
B	being serenaded	☐
C	shopping for souvenirs	☐
D	sampling the traditional food	☐
E	seeing famous paintings	☐
F	sunbathing on the beach	☐
G	taking a boat trip	☐

(3 marks)

Test: Listening 2

Listen to the recording

School activities

1 Your Spanish friends are telling you about the school activities they are involved in.

What do they do?

Listen to the recording and put a cross [×] in each one of the **three** correct boxes.

A	plays in an orchestra	☐
B	is a member of the chess club	☐
C	takes part in plays and shows	☐
D	serves in a snack bar	☐
E	trains with the athletics team	☐
F	sings in the choir	☐
G	is in the football team	☐

(3 marks)

Listen to the recording

Directions

2 You are listening to your Spanish friend's voicemail giving you directions to her house.

Listen to the recording and complete the gaps in each sentence. Use a word or words from the box below. There are more words than gaps.

> station   square   next to   right
>
> car park   church   left   bridge   straight on
>
> opposite   road   near

(a) When you leave the .... you need to

turn ....

(b) At the crossroads, go .... and then cross the

....

(c) When you get to the ...., you're nearly there: my house

is .... the petrol station.

(6 marks)

Test: Listening 3

Weather report

Listen to the recording

1 You are listening to the weather forecast in northern Spain, trying to plan your week.

What sort of weather are you going to have?

Listen to the recording and put a cross [×] in each one of the **three** correct boxes.

A	hot	☐
B	snow	☐
C	wind	☐
D	cold	☐
E	rain	☐
F	fog	☐
G	hail	☐

(3 marks)

Problems with a hotel

Listen to the recording

2 You hear Señor Castillo talking to the receptionist in your hotel.

Listen to the recording and complete the sentences by putting a cross [×] in the correct box for each question.

(i) Señor Castillo wants to …

☐	**A** book a room.
☐	**B** change rooms.
☐	**C** pick up his room key.
☐	**D** check in.

(ii) He does not want …

☐	**A** a balcony.
☐	**B** a private sitting room.
☐	**C** the evening meal.
☐	**D** to overlook the street.

(iii) The receptionist offers him a room …

☐	**A** with a double bed and a balcony.
☐	**B** with a double bed and no balcony.
☐	**C** with single beds and a balcony.
☐	**D** with single beds and no balcony.

(iv) The room overlooks …

☐	**A** the grounds.
☐	**B** the lake.
☐	**C** the park next door.
☐	**D** the pool.

(v) The room that she offers …

☐	**A** is smaller than the others.
☐	**B** is available in an hour.
☐	**C** costs a little more.
☐	**D** includes breakfast in the price.

(5 marks)

Test: Speaking 1

Listen to the recording

Topic: At the tourist office

1   Instructions to candidates:

You are in the tourist office of a seaside town. The teacher will play the role of the tourist office employee and will speak first.

You must address the employee as *usted*.

You will talk to the teacher using the five prompts below.

- Where you see – **?** – you must ask a question.

- Where you see – **!** – you must respond to something you have not prepared.

Task

Usted está en una oficina de turismo en Galicia (España) con su familia hablando con el empleado / la empleada.

1   Sitios de interés – información

2   Región – mapa

3   **!**

4   Estancia en la ciudad – duración

5   **?** Excursiones – barco

> Spend about 12 minutes preparing the following role play, using the prompts below. Then listen to the teacher's part and answer in the pauses. Finally, listen to the sample answers in the answer section.

Listen to the recording

Topic: Hobbies and free time

2   Instructions to candidates:

You are talking to your Spanish friend about your free time. The teacher will play the role of the friend and will speak first.

You must address your Spanish friend as *tú*.

You will talk to the teacher using the five prompts below.

- Where you see – **?** – you must ask a question.

- Where you see – **!** – you must respond to something you have not prepared.

Task

Estás hablando con tu amigo/a español/a sobre tu tiempo libre.

1   Actividades con amigos (**dos** detalles)

2   Actividades en tus últimas vacaciones (**dos** detalles)

3   **!**

4   **?** Deberes – cantidad

5   **?** Pasatiempos favoritos

> Spend about 12 minutes preparing the following role play, using the prompts below. Then listen to the teacher's part and answer in the pauses. Finally, listen to the sample answers in the answer section.

Test: Speaking 2

School

Listen to the recording

1 Mira la foto y prepara las respuestas a los siguientes puntos:

- la descripción de la foto
- tu asignatura favorita y por qué
- los mejores aspectos de tu instituto
- lo que hiciste en tu última clase de español
- cómo vas a prepararte para los exámenes

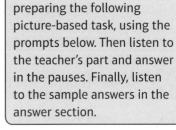
Spend about 12 minutes preparing the following picture-based task, using the prompts below. Then listen to the teacher's part and answer in the pauses. Finally, listen to the sample answers in the answer section.

Listen to the recording

2 Mira la foto y prepara las respuestas a los siguientes puntos:

- la descripción de la foto
- las presiones de los estudios
- lo que hiciste en tu última clase de español
- una cosa de tu instituto que te gustaría cambiar y por qué
- !

Test: Reading 1

Social media and technology

1 Read these comments on a Spanish website about the best aspects of technology.

Lorena	Lo mejor es la cantidad de información a la que puedes acceder. Si se te ocurre una pregunta, no tienes que pasar tiempo tratando de recordar la respuesta, sólo haces clic y la red te da lo que buscas.
Alejandro	Para mí es el sentido de estar conectado a toda hora. Si usas el correo electrónico o los mensajes en una red social, puedes comunicar en momentos con amigos en la próxima calle o familiares al otro lado del mundo.
Paula	El mejor aspecto para mí es la capacidad de crear obras de arte. Yo uso aplicaciones de diseño y es increíble lo que puedes producir a nivel casi profesional. Espero trabajar en diseño cuando termine mis estudios.
David	En mi opinión, lo más impresionante es la transformación en la manera en que escuchamos canciones. Es tan rápido descargarlas al móvil o al ordenador y en muchas ocasiones es muy barato.

Who says what?

Enter either **Lorena**, **Alejandro**, **Paula** or **David**. You can use each person more than once.

(a) .... is developing skills for a future career.

(b) .... loves the way the internet answers questions in seconds.

(c) .... uses it to listen to music.

(d) .... likes to keep in touch with people abroad.

(e) .... enjoys the creativity of certain software.

(f) .... remarks on the speed and the reasonable cost.   **(6 marks)**

Translation

2 Translate this passage **into English**.

> Si quiero comprar ropa, voy a la ciudad en tren o en autobús y mis amigos y yo vamos al centro comercial. El sábado pasado compré un regalo para mi madre porque es su cumpleaños.

....

....

....

....

....

....   **(12 marks)**

Test: Reading 2

Festivals

1   Read this article on a Spanish travel website about the Lanzada beach in Galicia.

> Existe una vieja tradición que tiene lugar cada Agosto, el último domingo del mes. Durante el resto de la temporada, la playa está llena de niños que juegan y sus padres que descansan. Sin embargo, este domingo especial las mujeres casadas que quieren tener un hijo vienen a bañarse en el mar. Según la leyenda, si la mujer se queda en el mar hasta que pasen nueve olas,* tendrá un hijo dentro del próximo año.

*ola = wave

Answer the following questions **in English**.

(a)   When does the tradition take place?

....   **(1 mark)**

(b)   Who takes part in the event? Give full details.

....   **(1 mark)**

(c)   What must they do to make their wish come true?

....   **(1 mark)**

(d)   What will then happen?

....   **(1 mark)**

Back to school

2   Read this extract from a letter from your Spanish friend. Put a cross [×] in the correct box.

> El profesor empezó por recordarnos las reglas del instituto (algunas tontas, algunas razonables) y luego nos dio el horario. Resulta que tengo física el viernes por la tarde, ¡qué horror! Quería dejarla pero tienes que estudiarla si quieres hacer ingeniería en el futuro. Tengo una clase de inglés a primera hora el lunes – no es el mejor momento para hablar un idioma extranjero cuando todavía tienes sueño.

(i)   Regarding the rules, your friend has …

A	a negative opinion.
B	found them very sensible.
C	mixed views.
D	no hope they will be followed.

(ii)   He comments that physics …

A	is not needed for his future career.
B	is not on his timetable.
C	is his favourite subject.
D	is his last lesson of the week.

(iii) The English lesson …

A	always sends him to sleep.
B	is not scheduled at the ideal time.
C	is first thing on Tuesday.
D	is taught by a native speaker.

(3 marks)

Test: Reading 3

The new teacher

1 Read this extract from *Historia de una Maestra* by Josefina Aldecoa where the new teacher meets her mixed-age class for the first time.

> Eran unos treinta. Me miraban inexpresivos, callados. En primera fila estaban los pequeños, sentados en el suelo. Detrás, en bancos con pupitres, los medianos. Y al fondo, de pie, los mayores. Treinta niños entre seis y catorce años, indicaba la lista que había encontrado sobre la mesa. Escuela unitaria, mixta, así rezaba mi destino. Yo les sonreí. «Soy la nueva maestra», dije, como si alguno lo ignorara, como si no hubieran estado el día antes acechando mi llegada. Recordaba al más alto, el del fondo. Parecía tener más de catorce años. Estaba medio subido a un árbol, cuando pasé ante él. Ahora me miraba en silencio.

Answer the following questions **in English**.

(a) Where were the little ones in the class? .... **(1 mark)**

(b) Where were the oldest ones? .... **(1 mark)**

(c) How old were the children? .... **(1 mark)**

(d) How did the new teacher try to put the children at their ease?

.... **(1 mark)**

(e) What did she conclude about the age of the tall boy?

.... **(1 mark)**

Translation

2 Translate this passage **into English**.

> Esta noche voy con mis padres a un concurso organizado por mi colegio para recaudar fondos para las víctimas del terremoto. Hay cuatro personas en cada equipo y tenemos que contestar preguntas sobre deporte, geografía, música y las noticias recientes. Espero que lo pasemos bien y que ganemos. El año pasado recolectaron más de ciento cincuenta euros.

....

....

....

....

....

.... **(12 marks)**

Test: Reading 4

Problemas medioambientales

1   Lee esta página web de un grupo ecologista sobre problemas en los meses recientes.

● ● ●	
Julio	Un escape de líquido peligroso de una fábrica química se encontró en el agua potable de cientos de casas en el pueblo de Martorell. Los habitantes protestaron delante del ayuntamiento sobre los riesgos de vivir al lado de esta fábrica.
Septiembre	Otro verano sin lluvias dejó muchas regiones en un estado avanzado de sequía. La tierra era amarilla y seca y muchos granjeros vieron las frutas y verduras devastadas.
Noviembre	El gobierno reveló que el consumo de electricidad había subido otra vez y dedicó más dinero a la investigación de recursos naturales sostenibles para reemplazar el carbón y el petróleo.

¿Cuándo ocurrieron estos acontecimientos? Escribe **julio**, **septiembre** o **noviembre**. Puedes usar cada palabra más de una vez.

(a)   En .... varios hogares se vieron afectados por la
      contaminación industrial.   **(1 mark)**

(b)   En .... anunciaron otro aumento en el consumo de energía.   **(1 mark)**

(c)   En .... los agricultores perdieron muchos cultivos.   **(1 mark)**

(d)   En .... los residentes se quejaron ante las autoridades.   **(1 mark)**

Food preferences

2   You read these entries in an online forum about favourite food.

● ● ●	
Sofía	¡Lo que a mí me encantan son los postres! Me gustan los helados, las tartas y todo tipo de pastelería, ¡aunque sé que no son nada buenos para la salud! Debería comer más fruta, pero la odio.
Gustavo	Para mí, lo peor son las hamburguesas: no son sabrosas en absoluto. Yo prefiero la comida casera de mi padre. Hace platos riquísimos con especias e ingredientes exóticos. ¡En mi casa nos gusta lo picante!
Pedro	Hoy en día cocino más que nunca con las verduras y las legumbres. Son muy variadas y hay muchas maneras deliciosas de prepararlas. Prefiero evitar los platos ricos con salsas o cremas.

Who says what about food?

Enter either **Sofía**, **Gustavo** or **Pedro**. You can use each person more than once.

(a)   .... avoids rich, creamy dishes.   **(1 mark)**

(b)   .... prefers spicy food.   **(1 mark)**

(c)   .... likes preparing vegetarian food.   **(1 mark)**

(d)   .... would choose ice cream rather than strawberries.   **(1 mark)**

(e)   .... is unlikely to go to a fast-food restaurant.   **(1 mark)**

Test: Writing 1

La familia

1 Estás en España en un intercambio con esta familia. Pones esta foto en el blog del instituto.

Describe la foto **y** da tu opinión sobre la familia.

Escribe aproximadamente 20–30 palabras **en español**.

....

....

....

....   **(12 marks)**

Reservando alojamiento

2 Vas de vacaciones a España con tu familia.

Escribe una carta al hotel para hacer la reserva.

Menciona:

- duración de visita

- día y hora de llegada

- habitaciones – detalles

- comidas que quieres.

Escribe aproximadamente 40–50 palabras **en español**.

Estimado Señor:

....

....

....

....

....

Atentamente,   **(16 marks)**

Test: Writing 2

En el restaurante

1 Traduce las frases siguientes **al español**.

(a) I like fish.

.... **(2 marks)**

(b) The food here is very good.

.... **(2 marks)**

(c) I am not going to have ice cream, I prefer fruit.

.... **(2 marks)**

(d) I ate in a French restaurant last week.

.... **(3 marks)**

(e) I never eat meat because I am a vegetarian.

.... **(3 marks)**

Los idiomas

2 Traduce el texto siguiente **al español**.

> In my school the Spanish classes are fun and varied and we learn a lot about the language and countries where Spanish is spoken. It is very useful to know another language because it gives you more opportunities to work in other countries. I started Spanish in primary school and in the future I would like to learn Chinese too.

....

....

....

....

....

.... **(12 marks)**

Test: Writing 3

Visitando una ciudad

1 Tu amiga Patricia viene a visitarte y llega mañana.

Escribe un email a Patricia.

Debes mencionar los puntos siguientes:

- una visita a una ciudad que estás planeando
- cómo vais a viajar
- lo que podéis hacer allí
- el tiempo que hizo ayer.

Escribe aproximadamente 80–90 palabras **en español**.

....

....

....

....

....

....

....

....

....

....

....

....

....

....

....

....

....

....

....

....

.... **(20 marks)**

Had a go ☐   Nearly there ☐   Nailed it! ☐

Test: Writing 4

Las ambiciones para el futuro

1 Tu amigo Álvaro quiere saber tus planes para el futuro.

Escribe un email a Álvaro sobre lo que piensas hacer en el futuro.

Debes mencionar los puntos siguientes:

- tus opciones a los dieciséis años
- la opción que has escogido y por qué
- la experiencia laboral que has tenido
- el tipo de trabajo que te gustaría hacer.

Justifica tus ideas y opiniones.

Escribe aproximadamente 130–150 palabras **en español**.

....

....

....

....

....

....

....

....

....

....

....

....

....

....

....

....

....

....

....

.... **(28 marks)**

Answers

Identity and culture

1. Physical descriptions

1 B, C, F

2 (a) nose
   (b) hair
   (c) beard
   (d) mouth

2. Character descriptions

1 (i) B   (ii) B   (iii) A   (iv) D

2 Cuando era joven era un poco tímido/a y muy serio/a. Ahora soy más seguro/a de mí mismo/a y soy una persona responsable y optimista. Mis amigos dicen que soy amable y simpático/a.

3. Describing family

1 A Begoña and Pablo
   B Diego
   C Diego and Pablo
   D Marta
   E Lucía
   F Rosa and Gabriel
   G Gabriel

2 Gemma's parents have been divorced for eight years. Gemma has one sister and they live with their mother and stepfather. When their stepbrother visits for the weekend, Gemma has to share a room with her sister. They get on very badly with David.

4. Friends

1 (i)   C
   (ii) A
   (iii) A
   (iv) D

2 Describe esta foto.
   En la foto hay un grupo de jóvenes. Hay chicos y chicas y todos son buenos amigos. Creo que tienen quince o dieciséis años. Parecen muy felices y contentos.

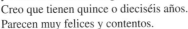

Listen to the recording

SPEAKING TRACK 100

   ¿Qué tipo de amigo/a eres tú?
   Creo que soy un buen amigo porque escucho a mis amigos y trato de ayudar si tienen problemas. Soy una persona tolerante y me llevo bien con mis amigos.

   Creo que el amigo/la amiga ideal debe apoyarte y ayudarte. ¿Qué opinas tú?
   Para mí, el amigo ideal debe tener un buen sentido del humor. También es importante tener cosas en común y hacer actividades juntos. El amigo ideal tiene que guardar tus secretos.

   ¿Cómo es tu mejor amigo/a?
   Es bastante alto con el pelo moreno. Es divertido y alegre pero puede ser tonto a veces. No es serio ni responsable pero es muy inteligente.

   ¿Qué actividades haces con tus amigos/as?
   Jugamos al fútbol en el parque y de vez en cuando vamos al cine. Los sábados vamos al polideportivo para jugar al bádminton y algunos fines de semana vamos de pesca.

5. Role models

1 A, D, E

2 A, F, G

6. Relationships

1 (a) Sofía se siente **enamorada**.
   (b) Sebastián se siente **triste**.
   (c) Mariana se siente **enfadada**.
   (d) Alejandro se siente **enamorado**.
   (e) Gabriela se siente **confusa**.

2 Role play
   Friend: ¿Tú y Miranda queréis salir con nosotros el sábado?
   You: Miranda no puede ir porque está ocupada el sábado.
   Friend: ¿Y tú, entonces? ¿Quieres salir conmigo y unos amigos?
   You: Sí, me gustaría mucho. No quiero pasar el día solo/a.
   Friend: ¿Adónde prefieres ir? ¿A la playa o a la montaña?
   You: Prefiero ir a la playa porque va a hacer muy buen tiempo.
   Friend: ¿Cómo te llevas con Miranda?
   You: Me llevo muy bien con ella.
   Friend: Pues fantástico. ¿Tienes una pregunta?
   You: ¿Cómo es tu relación con Miranda?
   Friend: Somos buenas amigas. Es como mi hermana.

Listen to the recording

SPEAKING TRACK 101

7. When I was younger

1 (a) he was an only child
   (b) (i) a desert island in the sea (ii) a tropical (rain)forest with wild animals
   (c) he didn't get good grades
   (d) he read a lot and he wrote (little) stories

2 B, D, E

8. Peer group pressure

1 (a) foolish
   (b) exciting
   (c) unpleasant
   (d) negative
   (e) different

2 **Model answer**: Mi amiga, Claire, es pequeña, delgada y morena con el pelo largo y liso. Es bastante tímida y no está muy segura de sí misma. Por eso, quiso ser más atrevida y empezó a salir con un grupo de chicas mayores un poco tontas. Descubrí que bebía mucho alcohol cuando salía con sus nuevas amigas y que se comportaba muy mal. Intenté hablar con ella y decirle la verdad sobre las chicas que eran sus amigas. Por suerte, me escuchó. Ahora no sale con esas chicas y nunca bebe alcohol.

9. Customs

1 (i) A   (ii) B   (iii) A   (iv) B

2 Describe esta foto.
   Hay un grupo de personas al lado de una hoguera. Es el cinco de noviembre, una fiesta en Gran Bretaña. Hay fuegos artificiales y un ambiente alegre.

Listen to the recording

SPEAKING TRACK 102

¿Qué costumbre celebras en tu casa? Explícala.
En mi casa la Navidad es una ocasión muy especial. Siempre hay muchos parientes en casa para Navidad porque mis abuelos, mis tíos y mis primos vienen a comer con nosotros. Abrimos los regalos por la mañana y entonces todo el mundo ayuda con la preparación de la comida.

¿Qué tipo de comida prefieres para una ocasión especial?
Me gusta mucho la comida italiana y para mi cumpleaños vamos a mi restaurante favorito para tomar pasta y bistec.

¿Qué piensas de las costumbres españolas?
Creo que las fiestas españolas son muy animadas y divertidas. También pienso que son bastante caras.

¿Crees que la siesta es una buena idea para tu país?
No, creo que la siesta no es una buena idea para mi país porque no hace calor aquí como en España y solo tenemos una hora para comer.

10. Everyday life

1   (a) gets up
    (b) read the paper or watch TV
    (c) goes to a friend's house or plays basketball in the park
    (d) watched a film on his laptop
    (e) angry / cross

2   **Model answer**: Los fines de semana me levanto bastante tarde, normalmente sobre las once. Los sábados como en una hamburguesería pero los domingos como en casa.

Los sábados juego al fútbol. Los domingos hago mis deberes y también juego a los videojuegos. El sábado pasado fui de compras al centro comercial.

11. Meals at home

1   (a) I have / she has been a vegetarian for 5 years.
    (b) I have / he has just prepared a fish soup.
    (c) We / they always sit at the table to eat.
    (d) I have not / he has not drunk coffee for 2 years.

2   Describe la foto.
    En la foto hay una familia comiendo en la mesa de la cocina. Son el padre, la madre y sus dos hijos, un niño y una niña. Están tomando pollo con ensalada y pan. Están bebiendo agua. Es una comida sana y la familia está contenta.

Listen to the recording

TRACK 103

¿Qué tomas típicamente en tu casa para comer?
En mi casa tomamos mucho espaguetis con salsa boloñesa. Es un plato italiano pero es muy popular en este país también. Mi padre lo hace muchas veces el viernes porque es rápido y sabroso.

¿A qué hora tomáis las comidas en casa?
En mi casa, tomamos el desayuno sobre las siete y media y la cena a eso de las seis. Los fines de semana, solemos desayunar más tarde y comer sobre la una.

¿Qué tomaste para comer el fin de semana pasado?
El sábado pasado tomamos filete con ensalada y patatas fritas pero no comimos postre. Estaba muy rico. El domingo, tomamos albóndigas con arroz y judías verdes. De postre había una tarta de manzanas deliciosa.

¿Qué tal la comida en tu instituto?
En mi instituto la comida es bastante aburrida. No hay mucha variedad y no es muy sana. Hay pizza y patatas fritas casi todos los días.

12. Food and drink

1   (a) sandwich
    (b) strawberry
    (c) omelette
    (d) pineapple

2   (a) pescado
    (b) carne
    (c) verduras
    (d) fruta
    (e) carne

3   I really like going for tapas because you can try a variety of dishes. In Galicia where I live the speciality is fish and last night I had seafood in a very tasty sauce.

13. Shopping for clothes

1   Elvira C
    Antonia B
    Pepito E

2   (a) They are too small
    (b) She looks in the shops and thinks
    (c) Online

SPEAKING TRACK 104

Listen to the recording

3   **Role play**
    Teacher (playing role of exchange partner Camila (female)): ¿Qué quieres hacer este sábado?
    You: Me gustaría ir de compras. Quiero comprar unas cosas para mi familia.
    Camila: ¿Adónde quieres ir de compras?
    You: Prefiero ir a un centro comercial porque hay mucha variedad y las tiendas son mejores.
    Camila: ¿Qué vas a comprar?
    You: Voy a comprar una pulsera y unos guantes.
    Camila: ¿A qué hora vamos?
    You: A las diez.
    Camila: Entonces vamos al centro comercial en la ciudad. ¿Tienes una pregunta?
    You: ¿Te gusta ir de compras?
    Camila: Me encanta.

14. Social media

1   (a) Jaime
    (b) Laura
    (c) Teo
    (d) Mariana
    (e) Jaime
    (f) Mariana

2   Me gusta usar las redes sociales para ver lo que hacen mis amigos y mirar las fotos que cuelgan. También algunos de los vídeos son realmente divertidos.

A veces pueden ser peligrosas porque algunas personas mienten sobre su edad y quiénes son. Nunca me quedarìa con alguien que conocí en Internet.

Anoche usé una red social para jugar a un juego durante veinte minutos y cuando hacía mis deberes, escribí una pregunta en la página de mi clase de geografía.

Este sábado voy a subir unas fotos de mis vacaciones recientes.

15. Technology

1 old / broken / tablet / mouse

2 **Role play**

Friend: ¿Cómo usas la tecnología?

You: Descargo música y busco información para mis deberes.

Friend: ¿Qué piensas de las tabletas?

You: Son un poco grandes para llevar.

Friend: ¿Te gusta jugar a juegos en Internet?

You: Sí, bastante. Hay algunos juegos buenos.

Friend: A mí también. ¿Qué piensas del coste de la tecnología?

You: Creo que es muy cara pero mandar mensajes es gratis.

Friend: Es verdad. ¿Tienes una pregunta?

You: ¿Cuál es tu página web favorita?

Friend: Me gustan los mapas. Son muy útiles.

SPEAKING TRACK 105 · Listen to the recording

16. The internet

1 (a) madre
  (b) Cristina
  (c) padre
  (d) Jorge
  (e) Cristina

2 B, E, G

3 I can't imagine life without the internet because in my house we usually use it every day. If you forget the name of a film or you want to know when a certain author was born, the internet has all the answers. Furthermore / In addition, the way in which we do our shopping / the way we shop is different now.

17. Pros and cons of technology

1 (i) B   (iv) D
  (ii) C   (v) A
  (iii) B

2 Describe esta foto.

En la foto hay una niña que mira la pantalla de un ordenador portátil. Parece preocupada y sorprendida. Creo que está navegando en Internet y ha encontrado una página inapropiada.

SPEAKING TRACK 106 · Listen to the recording

¿Qué piensas de los problemas de Internet?

Es fácil pasar demasiado tiempo en Internet cuando deberíamos estar haciendo cosas más activas o creativas. Hay problemas con la piratería y el fraude y personas que no son quienes dicen que son. También, el acoso cibernético es muy desagradable para las víctimas.

En tu opinión, ¿cuáles son los aspectos buenos de Internet?

Internet nos permite mantenernos en contacto con amigos y parientes y es una fuente casi infinita de información. Con Internet la comunicación es rápida y fácil y puedes ahorrar tiempo y dinero haciendo las compras en la red.

¿Qué hiciste en Internet anoche?

Anoche descargué unas canciones, mandé un ensayo a mi profesor por correo electrónico y charlé con mis amigos en la red. Fue muy útil porque organizamos un partido de fútbol.

¿Cómo vas a usar Internet este fin de semana?

Este fin de semana voy a usar unos sitios web que me ayudan a repasar para los exámenes. También jugaré a unos juegos en mi tiempo libre. Probablemente buscaré información para los deberes el domingo.

18. Hobbies

1 (a) Adela
  (b) Nicolás
  (c) Sara
  (d) Benjamín

2 **Model answer:** En mi tiempo libre hago atletismo y juego al tenis. También me gusta tocar la guitarra y dibujar. Hago atletismo los sábados y juego al tenis los domingos con mi hermano.

Me gustan los deportes porque son emocionantes y muy activos. Mis otros pasatiempos son relajantes y creativos.

19. Music

1 (a) Fernando
  (b) Eduardo
  (c) Eduardo
  (d) Fernando
  (e) David

2 (a) One of : He came here to study music / to improve his art (skills) / to get better opportunities.
  (b) (i) Breakfast is the best meal of the day.
      (ii) He has lots of fans. / He is having some success. / He has met some good musicians.
  (c) (i) He plays and writes songs.
      (ii) He has a rest and goes out.
  (d) His ideas for songs won't let him.
  (e) He does a concert or radio appearance.
  (f) To promote his music.

20. Sport

1 (i) B   (iv) C
  (ii) D   (v) A
  (iii) D

2 A, B, D

21. Reading

1 A, C, E

2 Describe esta foto.

En la foto hay una chica que está leyendo un libro electrónico. Está viajando en el tren y es muy útil pasar el tiempo con un libro porque es relajante.

SPEAKING TRACK 107 · Listen to the recording

¿Qué piensas de leer?

Me gusta mucho leer y me chiflan las novelas de fantasía. No tengo mucho tiempo para la lectura pero cuando estoy de vacaciones leo mucho.

Describe un beneficio de la lectura.

La lectura es buena para tu vocabulario y para tu imaginación. Cuando lees, puedes aprender mucho sobre otra gente y otros países.

¿Te gustan los libros electrónicos?

Me encantan los libros electrónicos, sobre todo cuando estoy de vacaciones, porque hay cientos de libros en un aparato y es bastante ligero.

¿Qué hiciste ayer para relajarte?
Ayer di un paseo en el parque con mi perro y también por la tarde leí un poco de una novela policíaca.

22. Films

1 A, C, D

2 (a) she has to study
(b) her parents won't let her
(c) they had a good time at the cinema / they laughed a lot
(d) the best moments of the film
(e) she did a dramatic impersonation of the leading actress

23. TV

1 B, D, E, G

2 (a) films
(b) documentaries
(c) soaps
(d) boring

3 **Model answer:** Me gusta ver la televisión por la tarde cuando termino los deberes. Es una buena manera de relajarme.

Mis programas favoritos son las comedias y las películas porque son más divertidas que las series.

No me gustan nada los realitys porque no son interesantes y detesto los concursos porque la gente es muy tonta.

Siempre veo los partidos de fútbol en la televisión con mi familia porque nos gusta mucho el deporte y el fútbol es muy emocionante.

24. Celebrations

1 (a) Paula
(b) Emilio
(c) Beatriz
(d) Paula
(e) Santi
(f) Emilio

2 A, C, G

25. Festivals

1 (a) She protects / looks after everyone associated with the sea, even swimmers and windsurfers.
(b) To the port / harbour
(c) In a boat decorated with lights and flowers
(d) On a trip round the bay
(e) Music and a procession of boats

2 A, E, F

Local area, holiday and travel

26. Holiday preferences

1 B, D, F

2 (i) C   (ii) A   (iii) C   (iv) B

27. Hotels

1 (a) Begoña
(b) Andrea
(c) David
(d) Carlos

2 (a) It's cheaper and the room is bigger.
(b) C, E, G
(c) One

28. Camping

1 (i) C   (ii) A   (iii) A   (iv) B

2 **Role play**
Employee: Buenos días. ¿En qué puedo ayudarle?
You: Quisiera reservar una parcela en el camping para cuatro personas y una tienda.
Employee: ¿Para cuántas noches y en qué fechas?
You: Para diez noches. Vamos a llegar el 30 de julio.
Employee: Muy bien. ¿De qué nacionalidad son ustedes?
You: Somos irlandeses.
Employee: ¿Quiere algo más?
You: Sí. Quiero alquilar una bicicleta.
Employee: Muy bien. Tenemos muchas. ¿Tiene una pregunta?
You: ¿Qué instalaciones hay en el camping?
Employee: Les mandaré un folleto con todos los detalles.

Listen to the recording
SPEAKING TRACK 108

29. Accommodation

1 (a) Maruja
(b) Pablo
(c) Pili
(d) Juli

2 (a) campsite in Italy
(b) cousin's house / house in Barcelona
(c) youth hostel in the country
(d) hotel on the coast

30. Holiday destinations

1 (a) Luisa
(b) Rahesh
(c) Li Jun
(d) Luisa

2 (a) coast
(b) city / town
(c) mountains
(d) country(side)
(e) theme park

31. Travelling

1 (a) give him a lift / pick him up
(b) buy her a ticket
(c) his train is delayed
(d) change trains twice
(e) during the day

2 **Role play**
Friend: ¿Cuándo vas a llegar?
You: Voy a llegar el diez de agosto a las once.
Friend: ¿Cuáles son los detalles de tu llegada?
You: Viajo en tren y llego a la estación en el centro.
Friend: ¿Qué equipaje tendrás?
You: Tendré una mochila y una bolsa.
Friend: Vivo bastante lejos de la estación.
You: ¿Cómo voy a llegar a la casa?
Friend: Lo mejor sería coger un taxi.
You: ¿Cuánto cuesta un taxi a la casa?
Friend: Solo cuatro o cinco euros.

Listen to the recording
SPEAKING TRACK 109

32. Holiday activities

1 (a) Ali
   (b) Mario
   (c) Daniela
   (d) Tanvi
   (e) Daniela
   (f) Ali

2 (i) B   (iv) C
   (ii) D   (v) B
   (iii) A

33. Holiday experiences

1 (i) C, E, G
   (ii) the beach is bigger than it looks in the photos
   (iii) it is very tasty

2 B, D, F, G

34. Transport and directions

1 (a) turn right
   (b) cross the bridge
   (c) the second street on the left
   (d) Church Square / the square
   (e) the post office
   (f) opposite the hairdresser's

2 **Model answer:** Normalmente, cuando hace sol, voy al instituto a pie porque no está muy lejos. Pero si llueve, mi madre me lleva en coche.

   Cuando vamos de vacaciones, me gusta ir en avión porque es directo. Es mucho más rápido que ir en barco.

   En mi región, los pueblos tienen una red de autobuses para llegar a la ciudad, y en la ciudad los trenes van a todas partes del país. El sistema es bueno.

   Para mantenerme en forma voy a ir en bicicleta a las tiendas o a la casa de mis amigos.

35. Transport problems

1 (a) car
   (b) petrol
   (c) breakdown
   (d) missed
   (e) close

2 **Role play**
   Police officer: ¿Dónde estaba usted cuando vio el accidente?
   You: Estaba aquí en el cruce, delante de la tienda de comestibles.
   Police officer: ¿Qué pasó?
   You: Hubo un accidente entre dos coches.
   Police officer: ¿Quién causó el accidente?
   You: Creo que el conductor del coche rojo iba demasiado rápido
   Police officer: Entiendo. ¿Tiene una pregunta?
   You: ¿Hay muchos accidentes aquí?
   Police officer: No, esta es la primera vez. ¿Tiene otra pregunta?
   You: ¿Cuántas personas estaban en los coches?
   Police officer: Sólo dos y ambos están bien.

36. Holiday problems

1 (a) It's too small to sit on.
   (b) The heat in the bedroom is unbearable.
   (c) The air conditioning is broken.
   (d) There are no towels and it's not very clean.
   (e) It has nice/pretty gardens and a good restaurant.
   (f) By changing apartment.

2 (a) La ducha no funciona. / No funciona la ducha.
   (b) No hay sábanas en la cama.
   (c) Me hacen falta / Me faltan / Necesito dos toallas en el (cuarto de) baño.
   (d) Visité la ciudad ayer y perdí mi pasaporte.
   (e) El (cuarto de) baño no está muy limpio y falta jabón.

37. Asking for help abroad

1 (a) umbrellas
   (b) earrings
   (c) mobile phones
   (d) keys
   (e) watches

2 (a) in her bag / handbag
   (b) yesterday evening / last night
   (c) black leather
   (d) it contains a photo of her husband
   (e) fill in a form

38. Eating in a café

1 B, C, G

2 **Role play**
   Friend: ¿Qué quieres tomar?
   You: Quiero un café con leche.
   Friend: ¿Quieres comer algo?
   You: Me gustaría una hamburguesa.
   Friend: ¿Qué bebes normalmente cuando estás en casa?
   You: Bebo zumo de naranja.
   Friend: ¿Qué piensas de la comida española?
   You: Es muy rica.
   Friend: Me alegro. ¿Tienes una pregunta?
   You: ¿Cuánto cuesta?
   Friend: Nada. Te invito yo.

Listen to the recording TRACK 111

3 **Model answer:** En la foto mi hermana y sus amigos están en un café. Mi hermana come tarta, su amigo toma un café y su amiga come tarta también.

39. Eating in a restaurant

1 (a) salad
   (b) (potato) omelette
   (c) spaghetti
   (d) peach
   (e) chicken

2 C, D, F

40. Shopping for food

1 (a) on the kitchen table
   (b) half a kilo
   (c) market
   (d) bananas
   (e) (the box of) biscuits
   (f) 4 slices
   (g) a can/tin of beans

2 **Role play**
   Shop assistant: Buenos días. ¿En qué puedo ayudarle?
   You: Quiero unas fresas.
   Shop assistant: ¿Cuántos kilos quiere?
   You: Deme medio kilo.
   Shop assistant: Muy bien. ¿Algo más?
   You: Sí, una botella de agua mineral.
   Shop assistant: Aquí tiene.

Listen to the recording TRACK 112

You: También quiero cuatro lonchas de queso.
Shop assistant: Muy bien. ¿Tiene una pregunta?
You: Sí, ¿cuánto es?
Shop assistant: Cuatro con veinte.

41. Buying gifts

1. (a) barato
   (b) cumpleaños
   (c) ropa
   (d) joyas
   (e) librería

2. (a) Lorena
   (b) Patricia
   (c) Elena
   (d) Patricia
   (e) Elena
   (f) Lorena

42. Opinions about food

1. (i) B
   (ii) A
   (iii) D
   (iv) B
   (v) C

2. Me gusta mucho la comida española y el restaurante cerca de la plaza hace comida buenísima. El pescado es muy rico / sabroso y me encantó la salchicha picante que tomé / comí la semana pasada. La comida siempre es apetitosa y, en mi opinión, es bastante sana. Vamos a comer allí el viernes.

43. The weather

1. (a) sur
   (b) oeste
   (c) este
   (d) oeste
   (e) norte

2. I live in the north-west of Spain and the climate here is not as hot as in the south. In summer the weather is good but the sun does not shine every day. We have had a rainy weekend.

44. Places to see

1. (a) Just out of town; a 20-minute walk away.
   (b) It's one of the oldest in the country.
   (c) It was voted best in the north.
   (d) What life was like a hundred years ago.
   (e) Behind the town hall.
   (f) To the left of the library.

2. Describe esta foto.
   Es una ciudad en la costa con muchos edificios muy altos. También hay una plaza de toros y barcos en el puerto. Hay árboles verdes en las montañas y el mar es muy azul.

Listen to the recording

   Me gusta mucho visitar ciudades en otros países. ¿Y a ti?
   Sí, es muy interesante. Las tiendas son diferentes y me gusta visitar los monumentos.

   ¿Adónde van los turistas cuando visitan tu región?
   Van a las ciudades grandes para experimentar la cultura y visitar los museos y galerías. También van a las montañas y los lagos.

   ¿En qué ciudad te gustaría más vivir y por qué?
   Me gustaría vivir en Barcelona porque hace buen tiempo

y el club de fútbol es uno de los mejores del mundo. También hay una playa bonita y un acuario interesante.

¿Qué visitaste en tus últimas vacaciones?
Fuimos a Londres un fin de semana y visitamos el palacio de Buckingham. También fuimos al teatro para ver un espectáculo de música y fuimos en barco por el río.

45. Tourist information

1. (a) a (street) map of the town
   (b) next to the church
   (c) the other side of the bridge
   (d) it opens at ten
   (e) the times the boat trips go; the routes they follow
   (f) a guided walking tour of the town

2. **Employee:** Buenos días. ¿En qué puedo ayudarle?
   You: Quisiera información sobre los sitios de interés en la ciudad.

Listen to the recording

   Employee: Aquí tiene.
   You: También me gustaría una lista de alojamiento.
   Employee: Muy bien. ¿Qué tipo de alojamiento prefiere usted?
   You: Quiero un hotel barato.
   Employee: Aquí tiene una lista de hoteles. ¿Algo más?
   You: Sí, necesito un horario de trenes.
   Employee: Lo siento, no tenemos. Hay que ir a la oficina de Renfe. ¿Tiene una pregunta?
   You: ¿Dónde está la estación?
   Employee: Enfrente del ayuntamiento.

46. Describing a town

1. (i) C
   (ii) D
   (iii) A
   (iv) C
   (v) B

2. **Model answer:** La ciudad empezó a prosperar a principios del siglo veinte con las minas de carbón y la industria textil, sobre todo el algodón.

   Hoy la gente trabaja en las tiendas en el centro o en la gran fábrica de comida en las afueras. Algunas personas viajan a las grandes ciudades cerca de aquí para trabajar.

   Tenemos una red de transporte muy buena con dos estaciones de tren y muchos autobuses. Es fácil llegar a las grandes ciudades.

   Hay varios parques y jardines bonitos que están llenos de flores y árboles.

47. Countries and nationalities

1. (a) Japanese
   (b) Dutch
   (c) Danish
   (d) German
   (e) Swedish
   (f) Belgian

2. C, E, G

48. Places to visit

1. (i) D   (iv) A
   (ii) B   (v) D
   (iii) C   (vi) C

2. **Model answer:** En mi ciudad hay un gran mercado dos veces por semana, una gran variedad de tiendas y un centro comercial popular. Hay muchas pequeñas calles en el barrio histórico con edificios antiguos y cafés bonitos.

Durante el día, se puede dar un paseo en el parque o hacer una excursión en bicicleta al lado del río.

Por la noche, se puede ir al cine o cenar en uno de los restaurantes. También hay conciertos en el teatro.

Un día podemos ir al estadio para ver un partido de fútbol.

49. Describing a region

1 (a) coast, fishing
   (b) mountains, snow
   (c) countryside, horse riding

2 **Friend:** ¿Cómo es tu ciudad?
   You: Es bastante industrial y se pueden ver fábricas y chimeneas en muchas partes pero también tiene un centro atractivo con tiendas bonitas y espacios verdes.

Listen to the recording

   Friend: ¿Sabes algo de la historia de tu región?
   You: Lo más importante en el pasado de la ciudad fue la industria de la lana porque aquí se estableció un mercado para vender y comprar la lana. Y la ciudad creció poco a poco.
   Friend: ¿Qué piensas de vivir aquí y por qué?
   You: Me gusta vivir aquí porque mi familia y mis amigos viven cerca, pero a veces pienso que me gustará vivir en una ciudad más grande donde hay más que hacer.
   Friend: Sí, entiendo eso. ¿Tienes una pregunta?
   You: ¿Cuál es la industria más importante en tu región?
   Friend: Tiene que ser el turismo. ¿Tienes otra pregunta?
   You: ¿Cuántos habitantes hay en tu ciudad?
   Friend: Hay unos quinientos mil.

School

50. School subjects

1 (a) It's practical.
   (b) very boring
   (c) easy
   (d) interesting
   (e) No, because she always gets bad marks.

      OR: No, because it's difficult to learn all the dates.

2 Describe la foto.
   En la foto hay tres estudiantes jóvenes, dos chicos y una chica. Están en una clase de informática y el profesor está explicando algo que ven en la pantalla de los ordenadores. Parecen contentos y creo que les gusta la clase.

Listen to the recording

   ¿Qué piensas de estudiar informática?
   Pienso que es importante estudiar informática porque es muy útil tener conocimiento de ordenadores en el mundo laboral. La gran mayoría de las empresas buscan un entendimiento de la tecnología.

   ¿Qué asignaturas te gustaban en el pasado?
   Antes, me interesaba mucho el arte dramático y era mi asignatura favorita. Me gustaba mucho la profesora y las clases eran muy divertidas y animadas.

   ¿Qué planeas estudiar en el futuro?
   Me gustaría estudiar la geografía. Será muy interesante aprender sobre la formación de la tierra y hay muchos programas y páginas web útiles que me ayudarán a entender los aspectos difíciles.

¿Qué asignatura te gusta menos y por qué?
No me gustan nada las matemáticas. No las entiendo en absoluto. Odio las clases porque no comprendo las explicaciones de la profesora. Voy a dejar las matemáticas tan pronto como sea posible.

51. School life

1 B, D, E

2 **Friend:** ¿Qué tipo de deberes tienes que hacer?
   You: A veces tenemos que buscar información en el ordenador y escribir notas. Otras veces tenemos que escribir un ensayo o hacer ejercicios de gramática.

Listen to the recording

   Friend: ¿Hay actividades o clubes para los alumnos?
   You: Sí, tenemos muchos. Hay un club de música, otro de arte dramático y yo soy miembro del club de ajedrez.
   Friend: ¿Cómo te preparas para los exámenes?
   You: Leo mis notas, practico escribiendo planes para ensayos y hago repaso en páginas web educativas.
   Friend: Yo también. ¿Tienes una pregunta?
   You: ¿Cómo es tu uniforme?
   Friend: No está mal. Llevamos pantalones negros o una falda negra con una camisa blanca, un jersey azul y la corbata del instituto. ¿Tienes otra pregunta?
   You: ¿Cómo te fue en los últimos exámenes?
   Friend: Bastante bien. Saqué buenas notas.

52. The school day

1 (i) A
   (ii) D
   (iii) C
   (iv) C
   (v) B

2 (a) (around) 7.45
   (b) school door/gate
   (c) 20 minutes
   (d) they have free afternoons
   (e) do sport / have piano lessons / do what they like

53. Comparing schools

1 C, D, F

2 (a) they start at nine
   (b) traffic jams and impatient people
   (c) all the buses and parents in cars arrive at the same time
   (d) registration / the teacher taking the register
   (e) drama and business studies
   (f) it was early
   (g) they get homework every day

54. Describing schools

1 (i) C
   (ii) A
   (iii) D
   (iv) C
   (v) B

2 Mi instituto es bastante viejo y tiene muchas aulas, tres laboratorios y un gimnasio. Está a diez minutos de mi casa a pie. Hace cinco años construyeron una biblioteca grande / una gran biblioteca que es muy moderna y tiene instalaciones buenas. El año que viene / El año próximo van a hacer nuevas canchas de tenis.

55. School rules

1 (a) Regla 4
   (b) Regla 1
   (c) Regla 1
   (d) Regla 3
   (e) Regla 2

2 **Model answer:** En mi instituto no se puede correr en los pasillos, lo que los alumnos pequeños suelen hacer. Otra cosa prohibida es el chicle porque causa manchas desagradables y algunas personas dejan papeles por el suelo.

Los alumnos deben respetar a los profesores y los otros estudiantes y tratar a todos con consideración y cortesía. No se tolera el acoso en absoluto y hay castigos severos.

Hay algunas reglas muy importantes que son esenciales para asegurar el progreso de los alumnos. Por ejemplo, no se permite hablar mientras el profesor está hablando. Esto es muy importante si quieres aprender.

La regla que encuentro estúpida es la necesidad de llevar uniforme. No lo tienen en otros países y no creo que afecte ni al éxito de los estudiantes ni a su comportamiento.

56. Problems at school

1 (a) Elisa
   (b) Isabel
   (c) Saleh
   (d) David
   (e) failed nearly all
   (f) medicine and engineering

2 Many students say that there is a high level of pressure in schools in modern society. They think that it is only acceptable to get the best grades and to study the most academic subjects. Some schools have organised sessions after class designed to reduce stress. These include swimming, boxing and a choir.

57. Primary school

1 C, E, G

2 Describe esta foto.
   En la foto hay una clase de niños en uniforme azul con su profesora. Ella es joven con el pelo largo y rubio y hace una pregunta. Una chica levanta la mano para contestar. En la pared hay muchos pósteres y hay mucho color.

Listen to the recording

¿Cómo eras cuando eras pequeño/a?
Era bastante creativa y siempre quería dibujar o crear cosas artísticas. También me encantaba escribir historias y cantar. Me comportaba bien en la escuela y tenía bastantes amigos.

¿Cómo era tu profesor favorito o profesora favorita?
Un año tuve una profesora bastante mayor que era muy simpática y amable. Era como una abuela y trataba a sus alumnos con mucho cariño. La quería mucho y lloré cuando tuve que cambiar de clase.

¿Qué actividades te gustaban más?
Cuando era muy pequeña me acuerdo de jugar con el agua y con la arena. Era muy divertido y parecía que lo único que hacíamos era jugar. Más tarde, disfrutaba del periodo al final del día cuando la profesora nos leía una historia.

¿Cuáles eran tus asignaturas más fuertes?
El inglés me resultaba fácil y me encantaba hacer ejercicios de comprensión. También me gustaba la música y aprendí a tocar el teclado.

58. Success in school

1 (i) B
   (ii) C
   (iii) B
   (iv) D
   (v) A

2 **Friend:** ¿Cuál es la mejor manera de hacer los deberes?
   You: Es importante hacer los deberes cada tarde pero no cuando estás muy cansado.
   Friend: ¿Cómo deben comportarse en clase los estudiantes?
   You: Es esencial escuchar al profesor y escribir notas para recordarlo todo.
   Friend: ¿Qué haces si estás ausente y pierdes clases?
   You: Pido ayuda al profesor el día después.
   Friend: ¿Cómo te preparas para los exámenes?
   You: Hago un plan de repaso y luego estudio poco a poco cada día.
   Friend: Eso es una buena idea. ¿Tienes una pregunta?
   You: ¿Cómo haces el repaso?
   Friend: Uso las páginas web educativas.

59. School trips

1 B, C, G

2 **Model answer:** El mes pasado hicimos una excursión a la ciudad para ir al cine y a un restaurante español.

Viajamos en autocar desde el instituto y una vez en la ciudad fuimos a pie.

En el cine vimos una película española con una presentación y explicación de un profesor. Después fuimos a un restaurante español para tomar tapas y probar unos platos españoles típicos.

Me gustó mucho la visita. La película fue muy divertida y la comida fue muy rica. Espero volver al restaurante con mi familia.

60. School events

1 (a) autumn
   (b) band competition
   (c) Christmas
   (d) rugby championship
   (e) seven months

2 Describe esta foto.
   Es una orquesta de jóvenes que da un concierto en su instituto. Hay un grupo de estudiantes con sus instrumentos de música y todos están muy elegantes. Llevan muchos meses practicando y la profesora está muy contenta con ellos.

Listen to the recording

¿Qué actividades deportivas hay en tu instituto?
Tenemos partidos de fútbol y hockey todas las semanas y durante el verano hay campeonatos de tenis y de atletismo. A veces los profesores organizan torneos de baloncesto.

Describe un evento cultural en tu colegio.
Cada año organizan una exposición de todas las obras de arte de los estudiantes que hacen exámenes en dibujo. Los alumnos y profesores visitan durante el día y por la tarde los padres pueden venir a verla.

¿Qué evento te gustaría tener en tu instituto?
Quisiera tener un concurso de talentos para los estudiantes donde podríamos participar como cantantes, bailarines o músicos. Sería muy divertido.

¿Cómo has participado tú?
Participo en el coro porque me gusta mucho cantar. El mes pasado dimos un concierto donde cantamos algunas canciones clásicas pero también unas modernas. Fue estresante pero lo pasé bien al final.

61. School exchanges
1 (a) plane and coach / bus
   (b) 30 km from Barcelona
   (c) with a Spanish family
   (d) attend / take part in classes
   (e) trip to an ice rink
2 (i) C, D
   (ii) B, E

Future aspirations, study and work

62. Future plans
1 (a) Adrián
   (b) Lucía
   (c) Verónica
   (d) Lucía
   (e) Marcos
   (f) Adrián
2 (a) pocos
   (b) muchos
   (c) ninguno
   (d) todos
   (e) muchos

63. Future education plans
1 (i) A
   (ii) B
   (iii) D
   (iv) A
   (v) B
2 B, D, G

64. Using languages
1 A, B, F, G
2 Studying Spanish can open many doors at a professional level. There are many countries which have Spanish as their official language and therefore there are many jobs in which speaking the language may be an essential factor. Being able to speak Spanish can help you to enjoy literature and cinema. I started to learn Spanish two years ago.

65. Jobs
1 (a) Carlos
   (b) Juan
   (c) Ana
   (d) Juan
   (e) Laura
   (f) Juan

2 (a) mechanic, waiter
   (b) plumber, postal worker
   (c) teacher, journalist

66. Opinions about jobs
1 (a) bien pagado
   (b) aburrido
   (c) mal pagado
   (d) interesante
   (e) mal pagado

2 **Friend:** ¿Qué aspectos del trabajo son importantes para ti?
   You: Para mí, un trabajo tiene que ser variado y bastante bien pagado.
   Friend: ¿Qué tipo de trabajo no te gustaría hacer?
   You: No me gustaría trabajar en una oficina y hacer la misma cosa todos los días.
   Friend: A mí tampoco. ¿Qué piensas sobre trabajar en el extranjero?
   You: Me gustaría durante un tiempo pero sólo un año o dos.
   Friend: ¿Cuál sería tu trabajo ideal y por qué?
   You: Me encantaría ser ingeniera porque es un trabajo útil y creativo.
   Friend: Sí, es verdad. ¿Tienes una pregunta?
   You: ¿Crees que el dinero es importante en un trabajo?
   Friend: Bastante, pero no es lo más importante.

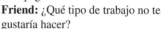
SPEAKING TRACK 121 · Listen to the recording

67. Applying for jobs
1 (a) double his current salary / double what he earns now
   (b) the way you dress; the way you shake hands / the way you give your hand
   (c) goes out to their car with them / accompanies them to their car
   (d) because a car tells you a lot about the owner
   (e) their car is full of rubbish

2 Soy creativo, trabajador y ambicioso y me llevo bien con otras personas / otra gente. Tengo experiencia como camarero en un restaurante y he trabajado como recepcionista en un hotel. Hablo español y un poco de francés y entiendo la importancia de las buenas relaciones con los clientes. El trabajo sería ideal para mí.

68. Work experience
1 A, C, E, G
2 (a) hospital
   (b) school
   (c) hotel
   (d) restaurant / café

69. Volunteering
1 (a) Carlos
   (b) Daniela
   (c) Begoña
   (d) Daniela

2 Describe esta foto.
   Es una foto de un grupo de personas que limpian la playa. Hay dos adultos y cuatro niños. Quitan la basura y la ponen en bolsas. Hace sol pero no mucho calor porque llevan chaquetas.

SPEAKING TRACK 122 · Listen to the recording

¿Cuáles son los beneficios del trabajo voluntario?
Hay muchos beneficios para la sociedad y también para el individuo. Muchas personas reciben ayuda, como la gente pobre o los ancianos, y también hay muchos beneficios para el medio ambiente.

¿Qué oportunidades hay para hacer trabajo voluntario en tu ciudad?
Siempre hay la oportunidad de ayudar en una residencia de ancianos o en una de las escuelas primarias. También, de vez en cuando, se organiza una recogida de desperdicios para limpiar el río o quitar la basura del bosque.

¿Qué experiencia de trabajo voluntario has tenido?
El año pasado trabajé varios fines de semana en una tienda con fines benéficos. Recibía las bolsas de ropa y libros que la gente llevaba y organizaba las cosas en la tienda. También servía a los clientes.

¿Qué ganaste con la experiencia?
Aprendí varias habilidades que podré utilizar en el mundo laboral. Por ejemplo, cómo relacionarme con la gente, cómo ser un miembro efectivo del equipo y cómo responder a las quejas de los clientes.

70. Helping others
1   B, E, F
2   **Model answer:** En la foto ayudo a mis padres con el trabajo de la casa. Lavo los platos y después voy a secarlos. No me importa ayudar porque mis padres trabajan mucho.

71. Charities
1   (i)   D
    (ii) B
    (iii) A
    (iv) B
    (v)   C

2   **Friend:** ¿Para qué asociaciones organizas eventos benéficos en tu instituto?
    You: Muchas veces recaudamos dinero para ayudar con la investigación científica de ciertas enfermedades, y en otras ocasiones nos gusta ayudar en causas medioambientales.
    Friend: ¿Qué tipo de actividades organizas?
    You: Hemos organizado un baile para los padres y profesores para recaudar fondos y también un concierto de música con la orquesta y el coro.
    Friend: ¿Cuánto dinero recaudas en general?
    You: Depende de la actividad pero normalmente entre ochenta y ciento veinte libras.
    Friend: No está mal. ¿Tienes una pregunta?
    You: ¿Qué eventos organizas en tu instituto?
    Friend: Lavamos los coches de los profesores y vendemos pasteles que hemos hecho. ¿Tienes otra pregunta?
    You: ¿Cuál es tu organización benéfica favorita y por qué?
    Friend: Me gusta ayudar a Oxfam porque hacen mucho trabajo para ayudar en países muy pobres.

72. Careers and training
1   (a) IT technician
    (b) he likes the idea of solving a company's IT problems; he wants to create solutions to improve their systems
    (c) A level / bachillerato in IT
    (d) a (shorter) training course with qualifications accepted in the industry
    (e) you don't get paid
    (f) Where is the best place to look for job adverts in the profession?

2   B, D, G

73. Messages
1   (a) phone back in ten minutes
    (b) wait / don't hang up
    (c) a pen to write down a number
    (d) 934756
    (e) if you / I want to leave a message

2   (a) Cristóbal
    (b) Delia
    (c) Begoña
    (d) Adrián
    (e) Begoña
    (f) Begoña

74. Part-time jobs
1   A, B, E

2   **Friend:** ¿Dónde trabajas y cuándo?
    You: Trabajo en un café en el centro de la ciudad los sábados.
    Friend: ¿Qué trabajos haces allí?
    You: Sirvo a los clientes, quito las mesas y lavo los platos.
    Friend: ¿Qué piensas del trabajo?
    You: Me gusta tratar con la gente y en general es divertido, pero no me gusta lavar los platos.
    Friend: Ya me imagino. ¿Tienes una pregunta?
    You: ¿Cómo llegas a tu trabajo?
    Friend: Cojo el autobús. ¿Tienes otra pregunta?
    You: ¿Cuánto ganas?
    Friend: Cincuenta euros al día.

75. Money
1   (a) parents and other family members
    (b) It has gone up more than 50% (compared to other times).
    (c) entertainment activities
    (d) Parents and grandparents are buying more products for the children.

2   **Friend:** ¿Cuánto dinero recibes como paga?
    You: Recibo quince libras a la semana.
    Friend: ¿Quién te da el dinero y cuándo?
    You: Mis padres y mi abuela me lo dan cada viernes.
    Friend: ¿Cuánto dinero intentas ahorrar?
    You: Normalmente pongo tres libras en el banco.
    Friend: ¿Qué te gusta comprar con tu dinero?
    You: Suelo comprar revistas, caramelos y saldo para mi móvil.
    Friend: Yo también. ¿Tienes una pregunta?
    You: ¿Piensas que recibes bastante paga?
    Friend: Sí, estoy contento con mi paga.

International and global dimension

76. Sporting events

1 (a) scored a goal
   (b) the boys were watching them
   (c) one nil
   (d) because the other team were much better than theirs/hers
   (e) to calm down

2 (i) A
   (ii) C
   (iii) B

77. Music events

1 (a) Iván
   (b) Celia
   (c) Raúl
   (d) Lidia
   (e) Celia
   (f) Iván

2 B, C, F

78. Green issues

1 (a) Tierra
   (b) Global
   (c) Mundo
   (d) Planeta
   (e) Global

2 C, E, F

79. Environmental action

1 (a) Miguel
   (b) Ana
   (c) Pilar
   (d) Pilar
   (e) Miguel
   (f) José

2 (a) marine animals and birds / sea life
   (b) fishermen and tourists
   (c) plastic bottles and containers
   (d) they end up trapped in bottles

80. Global issues

1 (a) Almost 900 million people
   (b) Health and education
   (c) To fight against world poverty
   (d) We need to understand the causes of poverty

2 A, C, F

81. Natural resources

1 (i) D
   (ii) C
   (iii) B
   (iv) A
   (v) D

2 Describe esta foto.
   En la foto hay un chico que tira basura en un contenedor. El chico tiene una botella de plástico que pone en el contenedor correcto. Normalmente hay otros contenedores para la ropa o el vidrio por ejemplo.

Listen to the recording

¿Qué se hace en tu instituto para ayudar al medio ambiente?
Tenemos que apagar las luces y los ordenadores al final del día. También se debe evitar el malgasto del papel escribiendo en los dos lados.

¿Reciclas mucho en tu casa?
Sí, reciclamos los restos de comida, el plástico, las latas, el vidrio y el cartón. Tenemos contenedores separados para todas estas cosas.

¿Cómo se puede evitar el malgasto del agua?
Tienes que cerrar el grifo cuando te cepillas los dientes, ducharte en lugar de bañarte y usar agua de lluvia en las plantas y las flores.

¿Cómo se puede reducir el uso de la electricidad en casa?
Es importante apagar todos los aparatos como la televisión y la consola de videojuegos. También puedes bajar la calefacción y ponerte un jersey.

Grammar

82. Nouns and articles

1 (a) la (b) el (c) las (d) los (e) la (f) el (g) las (h) los (i) el (j) la

2 (a) las (b) un (c) el (d) los (e) una (f) un (g) el (h) El

3 (b) Mi padre es ~~un~~ dentista y mi madre es ~~una~~ enfermera.
   (c) Hay muy pocos estudiantes en el instituto sin ~~un~~ móvil.
   (d) Escribo con ~~un~~ lápiz en mi clase de matemáticas.
   (e) En el futuro me gustaría ser ~~una~~ actriz.
   (h) Se puede reservar dos habitaciones con ~~una~~ ducha.

83. Adjectives

1 (a) cómoda (b) traviesos (c) rojo (d) interesantes (e) español (f) simpáticas (g) preciosa (h) baratos

2 (a) lujoso (b) cómodos (c) bueno (d) impresionante (e) limpia (f) útiles

3 (a) En Inglaterra hay **poca** gente que habla muy bien griego.
   (b) Lo mejor es que tiene un jardín **bonito**.
   (c) Estamos **contentas** porque hace buen tiempo.
   (d) En el futuro habrá una **gran** estatua aquí en la plaza.
   (e) Nuestro apartamento está en el **primer** piso.

84. Possessives and pronouns

1

English	Spanish singular	Spanish plural
my	mi	**mis**
your	**tu**	tus
his / her / its	**su**	**sus**
our	**nuestro / nuestra**	nuestros / nuestras
your	**vuestro / vuestra**	**vuestros / vuestras**
their	su	sus

2 (a) Mi (b) Su (c) Sus (d) Mis (e) Su

3 (a) el mío (b) las suyas (c) el nuestro (d) el tuyo

4 (a) María tiene un gato que es negro y pequeño.
   (b) Vivimos en un pueblo que está en el norte de Inglaterra.
   (c) En la clase de literatura tengo que leer un libro que es muy aburrido.

85. Comparisons

1   (a) Mi madre es **más alta que** mi padre.
    (b) Mariela es **menos paciente que** Francisco.
    (c) Este autobús es **más lento que** el tren.
    (d) La fruta es **tan sana / saludable como** las verduras.
    (e) Esta camisa es **tan cara como** aquella chaqueta.

2   (a) el mejor (b) los peores (c) la más pequeña (d) los más inteligentes (e) las menos aburridas

3   (a) Mi primo/a es más fuerte que tu tío.
    (b) Su móvil es pequeñísimo.
    (c) El examen de español es facilísimo.
    (d) Las películas de terror son tan emocionantes como las películas de acción.
    (e) ¡Mi instituto es el más feo!
    (f) Las ciencias son menos aburridas que la geografía.
    (g) Kylian Mbappé es el mejor.

86. Other adjectives

1

Masc sing	Fem sing	Masc plural	Fem plural	Meaning
este	**esta**	**estos**	**estas**	this / these
ese	esa	**esos**	**esas**	that / those
aquel	**aquella**	aquellos	**aquellas**	that (over there) / those (over there)

2   (a) estas botas (b) esta camiseta (c) aquella chica (d) esos plátanos (e) ese móvil (f) aquellas revistas (g) este libro (h) esa película (i) aquel tren (j) estos sombreros (k) esas fresas (l) aquellos chicos

3   (a) cada (b) misma (c) algunas (d) todos (e) otra

4   (a) Todos (b) Algunos (c) Todos (d) algunos (e) misma (f) mismos

87. Pronouns

1

yo	I
tú	you singular
él	he
ella	**she**
nosotros	we (masc.)
nosotras	**we (fem.)**
vosotros	**you plural (masc.)**
vosotras	you plural (fem.)
ellos	**they (masc.)**
ellas	they (fem.)

2   (a) Las hemos perdido.
    (b) La han perdido.
    (c) Teresa lo come.
    (d) Lo compro.
    (e) No la bebo.
    (f) No la lavo.
    (g) Lo quiero escribir. / Quiero escribirlo.
    (h) No quiero leerla. / No la quiero leer.
    (i) La necesito ahora.
    (j) Vamos a venderla. / La vamos a vender.

3   (a) I am going to write to him / her this afternoon.
    (b) I visited them yesterday.
    (c) I will do it if I have time.
    (d) I gave him / her a present for his / her birthday.
    (e) Have you seen them?

    (f) Vino a visitarme en casa. / Me vino a visitar en casa.
    (g) Me mandaron la reserva.
    (h) Voy a comprarlos en línea. / Los voy a comprar en línea.

88. The present tense

1   (a) vivimos (b) bailan (c) vendo (d) lleváis (e) odias (f) come (g) salimos (h) escucha

2   (a) comen (b) vivimos (c) tienes (d) hablan (e) debe (f) grita (g) chateo (h) lee (i) piensa (j) Podéis

3   (a) cenamos (b) trabajan (c) desayuno (d) pone (e) compramos (f) cuestan (g) Quiero (h) piden

89. Reflexive verbs (present)

1

me	afeito
te	afeitas
se	afeita
nos	afeitamos
os	afeitáis
se	afeitan
me	visto
te	vistes
se	viste
nos	vestimos
os	vestís
se	visten

2   (a) se (b) se (c) te (d) se (e) se (f) Nos (g) Os (h) Te

3   Todos los días Olivia **se levanta** temprano para ir a trabajar. **Trabaja** en una tienda de ropa famosa. Primero **se lava** los dientes y luego **se ducha** y **se viste**. **Baja** las escaleras y **desayuna** cereales con fruta. Siempre **se peina** en la cocina. Después, **se lava** la cara en el cuarto de baño que está abajo, al lado de la cocina. **Se pone** la chaqueta y **sale** a las ocho y media porque el autobús llega a las nueve menos cuarto. **Vuelve** a casa a las siete de la tarde.

90. Irregular verbs (present)

1   (a) conduce, conduzco
    (b) da, doy
    (c) oye, sale
    (d) hace, cojo
    (e) venís, traéis

2   (a) oye
    (b) conozco
    (c) vienen
    (d) cojo
    (e) vamos
    (f) sé
    (g) tienes
    (h) pongo
    (i) traigo
    (j) dicen

3   (a) Voy a España.
    (b) Tiene dos hermanas.
    (c) Oigo música.
    (d) Dice mentiras.
    (e) Cogemos el autobús.
    (f) Hacen los deberes.
    (g) Sales los sábados.
    (h) Doy clases.
    (i) Trae pan.
    (j) Pongo la mesa.

91. *Ser* and *estar*

1 (a) está (b) son (c) Soy (d) es (e) Son (f) está (g) Estáis (h) Estamos

2 (a) Where is the bank? ('estar' for location)
(b) My grandmothers are very generous. ('ser' for characteristics)
(c) I am from Madrid but I work in Barcelona. ('ser' for where you are from)
(d) The dress is green with white flowers. ('ser' for colours)
(e) It's four thirty in the afternoon. ('ser' for time)
(f) The wardrobe is opposite the door. ('estar' for location)
(g) You are (all) very sad today because the holidays have finished. ('estar' for moods)
(h) We are ready for the drama exam. ('estar' for meaning 'ready' not 'clever')

3 (a), (d), (e), (g) – ✓
(b) Mi amigo es inteligente y tiene el pelo negro.
(c) Me duele la cabeza y estoy enfermo.
(f) Mi madre es médica y mi padre es ingeniero.
(h) Mi casa es bastante pequeña – tiene solo un dormitorio.

92. The gerund

1 (a) comiendo – eating
(b) saltando – jumping
(c) corriendo – running
(d) tomando – taking (drinking/eating)
(e) durmiendo – sleeping
(f) asistiendo – attending
(g) escribiendo – writing
(h) escuchando – listening
(i) aprendiendo – learning
(j) pudiendo – being able to

2 (a) Está montando en bicicleta.
(b) Estoy escuchando música.
(c) Están navegando por Internet.
(d) Estamos viendo una película.
(e) Estás hablando con amigos.

3 (a) Estaba haciendo vela cuando llegó la tormenta.
(b) Estaban comiendo cuando su madre les llamó.
(c) Estábamos tomando el sol cuando empezó a llover.
(d) Estabas cantando cuando salió el tren.
(e) Estábamos viendo la tele cuando nuestro hermanastro volvió a casa.
(f) Estaba jugando a los videojuegos cuando llamó.
(g) Estabais escuchando al profesor cuando entró el perro.
(h) Estaba nadando en el mar cuando apareció el tiburón.

93. The preterite tense

1 (a) sacaron (b) volvimos (c) compró (d) llegaste (e) trabajasteis (f) fue (g) di (h) tuvimos (i) visitaron (j) bebió

2 (a) fui (b) tuvimos (c) dieron (d) fue (e) dio, pagué (f) fueron (g) dijo (h) fue (i) Hice (j) tuve

3 **Fui** al cine con mis amigos y **vimos** una película de acción. Después **comimos** en un restaurante italiano. **Comí** una pizza con jamón y queso, y mi amiga Lola **comió** pollo con pasta. **Bebimos** zumo de manzana y mi amigo Tom **comió** una tarta de chocolate pero yo no **comí** postre. Después del restaurante fui en tren a casa de mi prima. El viaje **fue** largo y aburrido. **Volví** a casa y **me acosté** a las once de la noche.

94. The imperfect tense

1 (b) De pequeños <u>nadábamos</u> en el mar todas las semanas. ✓
(c) <u>Había</u> mucha gente en el museo y las estatuas <u>eran</u> preciosas. ✓
(e) Cuando <u>eran</u> más jóvenes, no <u>comían</u> tomate ni lechuga.
(h) Me <u>ponía</u> nervioso cada vez que <u>hacía</u> una prueba de vocabulario. ✓
(j) <u>Nevaba</u> todos los días y <u>hacía</u> un frío horrible. ✓

2 (a) On Wednesday we went to the swimming pool and we swam for an hour and a half. (preterite for a completed action in the past)
(b) When we were kids, we used to swim in the sea every week. (imperfect for 'used to')
(c) There were lots of people in the museum and the statues were beautiful. (imperfect for descriptions)
(d) My father prepared a vegetarian supper for us. (preterite for a completed action in the past)
(e) When they were younger, they didn't eat tomatoes or lettuce. (imperfect to describe repeated actions in the past)
(f) Gabriela arrived in Madrid by train to start her new job. (preterite for a completed action in the past)
(g) Yesterday we met in the café and we talked all afternoon. (preterite for a completed action in the past)
(h) I used to get nervous every time I did a vocabulary test. (imperfect for 'used to')
(i) I had a great time because it was sunny and it didn't rain. (preterite for a completed action in the past)
(j) It snowed every day and it was terribly cold. (imperfect for descriptions)

3 (a) tenía (b) vivía (c) Estaba (d) pasé (e) trabajaban (f) gastó (g) comíamos (h) jugué

95. The future tense

1 (a) jugar (b) Va (c) a (d) voy (e) Vas (f) Vais (g) va (h) ir (i) vamos (j) Voy

2 (a) Vamos a ver la película.
(b) No trabajaré los lunes.
(c) Van a coger el metro.
(d) Irá a Inglaterra.
(e) Van a jugar con mi hermano.
(f) Irás a España.

3 (a) va a ir (b) voy a ir (c) voy a tomar (d) voy a tener (e) Voy a trabajar (f) Va a ser (g) voy a aprender (h) va a seguir (i) va a vivir

96. The conditional tense

1 (a) compraríamos – we would buy
(b) saldrían – they would go out
(c) trabajaríais – you (all) would work
(d) estaría – he / she / it would be
(e) jugarías – you would play
(f) vendríamos – we would come
(g) podrías – you could
(h) habría – there would be

2 (a) iría (b) tomarían (c) trabajaría (d) ganaríamos (e) habría (f) usaría (g) malgastarían (h) lucharían (i) ganaría (j) compartiríamos

3 NB All answers can use either podrías or deberías. Some answers are interchangeable.
(a) Podrías evitar el estrés.
(b) Podrías comer más frutas y verduras.
(c) Deberías hacer más ejercicio.

(d) Deberías ir al médico.

(e) Deberías acostarte temprano.

(f) Podrías ir al dentista.

(g) Deberías consumir menos energía.

(h) Podrías comprar ropa de segunda mano.

97. Perfect and pluperfect

1

	Perfect tense	Pluperfect tense	+ past participles
yo	he	**había**	
tú	**has**	**habías**	
él / ella / usted	**ha**	había	hablado
nosotros / nosotras	hemos	**habíamos**	comido
vosotros / vosotras	**habéis**	**habíais**	vivido
ellos / ellas / ustedes	**han**	habían	

2 (a) We have lost our car.

(b) Have you studied Spanish?

(c) They have bought a laptop.

(d) I have done my homework

(e) We have seen a very informative documentary.

(f) Me he roto el brazo.

(g) Han perdido la maleta.

(h) Hemos comido muchos caramelos.

(i) ¿Has visitado el museo hoy?

(j) Los azafatos han abierto las puertas.

3 (b) había perdido (c) había nadado (d) había hecho (e) había dejado (f) había encontrado

98. Giving instructions

1 (a) Dobla a la derecha.

(b) Cruza la plaza.

(c) Pasa el puente.

(d) Ten cuidado.

(e) Ven aquí.

(f) Canta más bajo.

(g) Lee en voz alta.

(h) Escucha bien.

(i) Pon la mesa.

(j) Haz este ejercicio.

2 (a) Doblad a la derecha.

(b) Cruzad la plaza.

(c) Pasad el puente.

(d) Tened cuidado.

(e) Venid aquí.

(f) Cantad más bajo.

(g) Leed en voz alta.

(h) Escuchad bien

(i) Poned la mesa.

(j) Haced este ejercicio.

3 (a) ¡Descarga la música!

(b) ¡Doblad a la izquierda!

(c) ¡Quita la mesa!

(d) ¡Haz la cama!

(e) ¡Pasad la aspiradora!

99. The present subjunctive

1 (a) hable (b) coman (c) vaya (d) vivas (e) trabajéis (f) salga (g) pueda (h) hagan (i) encuentre (j) seamos

2 (a) No comas este pastel.

(b) No compres aquel vestido.

(c) No tomes esa calle.

(d) No bebas un vaso de zumo de naranja.

(e) No veas esta película romántica.

(f) No firméis aquí.

(g) No rellenéis este formulario.

(h) No abráis las ventanas.

3 (a) escriban (b) haga (c) tengamos (d) sean (e) vaya (f) compren

100. Negatives

1 (a) No estudio geografía.

(b) No vamos a las afueras.

(c) Ricardo no compró una moto nueva.

(d) Sus padres no vieron la tele.

(e) No voy a ir a Francia la semana que viene.

2 1 E 2 D 3 B 4 G 5 A/F 6 A/F 7 C

3 (a) Mis profesores no enseñan nunca cómo repasar.

(b) En mi casa no tuvimos jamás una sala de juegos.

(c) No me he quemado nunca los brazos.

(d) Aquí no tengo ni vestidos, ni faldas, ni camisetas.

(e) No vas a comprar ningún coche.

(f) Mis padres no escuchan a nadie.

4 (a) Por la tarde nunca bebemos / tomamos café. / Por la tarde no bebemos / tomamos nunca café.

(b) No plancho, ni cocino, ni limpio.

(c) No hablan ningún idioma. / No hablan ningunos idiomas.

(d) No podemos hablar con nadie durante el examen.

(e) No fumaré jamás / nunca porque es una pérdida de dinero. / Jamás / Nunca fumaré porque es una pérdida de dinero.

101. Special verbs

1

me		I like
te	gusta (sing)	you like
le	gustan (plural)	he / she / it likes
nos		we like
os		you (all) like
les		they like

2 (a), (c) – ✓

(b) Nos **apetece** ir al cine mañana.

(d) No nos **gusta** la contaminación atmosférica.

(e) ¿Te **hacen** falta unas toallas?

3 (a) Nos hace falta un abrigo.

(b) Os encantan los caballos negros.

(c) A María le gustan aquellos zapatos.

(d) Te quedan veinte euros para comprar el regalo.

(e) Me duele la cabeza todo el tiempo.

(f) Les encantan los rascacielos porque son modernos.

102. *Por and para*

1 (a) For my birthday I want a new mobile phone.

(b) My friend works for an architect.

(c) Apps for the iPhone are incredible.

(d) I eat a lot of vegetables and fish in order to keep fit.

(e) You need the key to get into the house.

(f) Smoking is very bad for your health.

(g) They are going to organise a party to celebrate the end of the school year.

(h) For me, sports are always fun.

2 (a) El coche rojo pasó por las calles antiguas.

(b) Normalmente por la mañana me gusta desayunar cereales y fruta.

(c) Mandé la reserva por correo electrónico.

(d) Me gustaría cambiar este jersey por otro.

(e) En la tienda ganamos diez euros por hora.

(f) Había mucha basura por todas partes.

3 (a) Para (b) para (c) por (d) por / para (e) para

103. Questions and exclamations

1 Why? – **¿Por qué?**

What? – **¿Qué?**

When? – **¿Cuándo?**

How? – **¿Cómo?**

Where? – **¿Dónde?**

Where to? – **¿Adónde?**

Which? – **¿Cuál?**

Which ones? – **¿Cuáles?**

How much? – **¿Cuánto?**

How many? – **¿Cuántos?**

2

1	F
2	E
3	G
4	J
5	A
6	C
7	I
8	B
9	H
10	D

3 (a) horror (b) Cuánto (c) Cómo (d) guay (e) rollo

104. Connectives and adverbs

1 (a) rápidamente (b) difícilmente (c) lentamente
(d) alegremente (e) tranquilamente

2

1	L
2	E
3	A
4	K
5	D
6	B
7	G
8	J
9	F
10	I
11	C
12	H

3 (a) Sus padres cantan mal en la iglesia.

(b) No hablo mucho porque soy tímido.

(c) El tren pasa rápidamente por el túnel.

(d) Los pendientes son demasiado caros.

(e) A menudo comemos huevos por la mañana. /
Comemos a menudo huevos por la mañana.

(f) si / porque

(g) porque

(h) pero

105. Numbers

1 (a) veinte 20 (b) cuarenta y ocho 48
(c) nueve 9 (d) cien 100 (e) catorce 14
(f) mil 1,000 (g) trescientos 300 (h) cincuenta y siete 57
(i) veintitrés 23 (j) quince 15
(k) diecinueve 19 (l) quinientos 500

(m) un millón 1,000,000 (n) novecientos 900
(o) ochenta y ocho 88 (p) setenta y seis 76 (q) sesenta
y siete 67 (r) diez 10 (s) cero 0 (t) veintinueve 29

2 (a) mil novecientos noventa y nueve

(b) el diez de octubre

(c) el primero/uno de enero

(d) el tres de marzo

(e) dos mil trece

(f) el dieciséis de noviembre

(g) el treinta de mayo

(h) mil novecientos sesenta y ocho

(i) dos mil dos

(j) el veintiuno de abril

3 (a) Son las siete y cuarto.

(b) Es la una y veinticinco.

(c) Son las nueve menos veinticinco.

(d) Son las once y diez.

(e) Son las cuatro menos cuarto.

(f) Son las diez menos diez.

(g) Son las cinco y media.

(h) Son las doce.

Tests

106. Listening 1

1 (a) a sandwich (brought from home)

(b) spaghetti with tomato sauce

(c) (Spanish) omelette

2 B, E, G

107. Listening 2

1 B, D, E

2 (a) station, right

(b) straight on, bridge

(c) church, opposite

108. Listening 3

1 A, E, F

2 (i) B

(ii) D

(iii) C

(iv) A

(v) C

109. Speaking 1

1 **Employee:** Hola. ¿En
qué puedo ayudar?

You: Quisiera información
sobre los sitios de interés
en Cambados.

Employee: Este folleto será muy útil.

You: También quiero un mapa de
la región.

Employee: Muy bien. Aquí tiene. ¿Cómo prefiere viajar?

You: Prefiero viajar en autobús.

Employee: De acuerdo. ¿Cuánto tiempo van a estar aquí?

You: Vamos a estar aquí una semana.

Employee: ¡Qué bien! ¿Tiene una pregunta?

You: ¿Hay excursiones en barco?

Employee: Sí, aquí tiene una lista de viajes en barco.

SPEAKING TRACK 127

Listen to the recording

2 **Friend:** ¿Qué haces cuando sales con tus amigos?
You: Vamos de compras al centro y a veces al cine.
Friend: ¿Qué hiciste durante las últimas vacaciones?
You: Fui a la piscina varias veces y jugué al tenis con mi hermano.
Friend: ¿Qué pasatiempo te gustaría probar en el futuro?
You: Me gustaría aprender a tocar la guitarra.
Friend: Buena idea. ¿Tienes una pregunta?
You: ¿Recibes muchos deberes?
Friend: Hago dos horas de deberes cada día. ¿Tienes otra pregunta?
You: ¿Cuáles son tus pasatiempos favoritos?
Friend: Me gusta ir de pesca y hacer ciclismo.

Listen to the recording

110. Speaking 2

1 Describe esta foto.
En la foto hay una biblioteca en un instituto. Los estudiantes allí leen y estudian. Es una biblioteca moderna y tiene muchos libros.

Listen to the recording

¿Cuál es tu asignatura favorita y por qué?
Mi asignatura favorita es la historia porque las clases son muy variadas. En algunas clases hablamos y escuchamos y en otras leemos y escribimos.

¿Cuáles son los mejores aspectos de tu instituto?
Es un instituto muy bueno y los estudiantes son inteligentes. Los profesores son estrictos pero justos y nos ayudan mucho con nuestros estudios.

¿Qué hiciste en tu última clase de español?
Hicimos un ejercicio de comprensión sobre el medio ambiente y después trabajamos en grupos sobre unos ejercicios de gramática. También tuvimos un test de vocabulario.

¿Cómo vas a prepararte para los exámenes?
Voy a organizar un horario de repaso para mis asignaturas y voy a estudiar un poco cada día. También voy a usar las páginas web de repaso en Internet.

2 Describe esta foto.
Es la foto de la biblioteca de un instituto y hay varios alumnos leyendo allí. Los chicos llevan el uniforme negro y parecen muy ocupados. La biblioteca es grande y ordenada con muchos libros en los estantes. No hay ordenadores, sólo libros.

Listen to the recording

¿Cuál es tu opinión sobre las presiones de los estudios?
Ser estudiante puede ser muy estresante porque hay muchas asignaturas y quieres sacar buenas notas en todas. Hay muchos deberes y cuando hay exámenes es peor porque tienes que repasar todo. Es difícil encontrar tiempo para las actividades de ocio.

¿Qué hiciste en tu última clase de español?
Hicimos un ejercicio de comprensión sobre el medio ambiente y después trabajamos en parejas para hablar de las cosas que reciclamos. También tuvimos un test de vocabulario.

¿Qué te gustaría cambiar en tu instituto y por qué?
Me gustaría cambiar las opciones. Hay algunas asignaturas que me gustaría estudiar pero no se ofrecen en mi instituto y yo creo que serían muy populares. Por ejemplo, mis amigos y yo queremos estudiar empresariales pero no tenemos la oportunidad.

¿Te gustaría ser profesor/a y por qué o por qué no?
Creo que ser profesor tiene algunas ventajas como las vacaciones largas, y el salario no está mal. Sin embargo, también hay desventajas como tener que corregir los deberes cada tarde o tener chicos traviesos y maleducados en la clase.

111. Reading 1

1 (a) Paula
(b) Lorena
(c) David
(d) Alejandro
(e) Paula
(f) David

2 If I want to buy clothes, I go to town / to the city on the train or the bus and my friends and I go to the shopping centre. Last Saturday I bought a present for my mother because it is her birthday.

112. Reading 2

1 (a) the last Sunday in August
(b) married women who want to have a child
(c) stay in the sea until nine waves have passed
(d) they will have a child within the year

2 (i) C
(ii) D
(iii) B

113. Reading 3

1 (a) sitting on the floor at the front
(b) standing at the back
(c) between six and fourteen
(d) by smiling
(e) he looked over 14

2 This evening I'm going with my parents to a quiz organised by my school to raise funds for the victims of the earthquake. There are four people in each team and we have to answer questions on sport, geography, music and recent news. I hope we have fun and we win. Last year they collected more than a hundred and fifty euros.

114. Reading 4

1 (a) julio
(b) noviembre
(c) septiembre
(d) julio

2 (a) Pedro
(b) Gustavo
(c) Pedro
(d) Sofía
(e) Gustavo

115. Writing 1

1 **Model answer:** En la foto hay una familia. Come en el jardín porque hace buen tiempo. Hay bastante comida en la mesa, por ejemplo, carne, pan y una ensalada. Creo que es una familia feliz.

2   **Model answer:** Quisiera hacer una reserva para el sábado dos de julio para siete noches en total. Vamos a llegar sobre las once de la mañana. Queremos una habitación doble y una habitación individual con vistas al mar. También queremos balcón. No queremos cena, sólo desayuno.

116. Writing 2

1   (a) Me gusta el pescado.
     (b) La comida aquí es muy buena.
     (c) No voy a tomar helado, prefiero fruta.
     (d) Comí en un restaurante francés la semana pasada.
     (e) Nunca como carne porque soy vegetariano/a.

2   En mi instituto las clases de español son divertidas y variadas y aprendemos mucho sobre el idioma y los países donde se habla español. Es muy útil saber otro idioma porque te da más oportunidades de trabajar en otros países. Empecé español en la escuela de primaria y en el futuro me gustaría aprender chino también.

117. Writing 3

1   **Model answer:** ¡Hola Patricia! Durante tu visita vamos a pasar un fin de semana en Edimburgo en Escocia. Es una ciudad muy histórica y bonita con muchas atracciones. Vamos a viajar en tren porque hay un tren directo desde la estación en nuestro pueblo. Creo que el viaje es de una hora y media. En Edimburgo podemos visitar el castillo, ir de compras en la famosa calle central y comer en uno de los restaurantes de mariscos. De momento tenemos buen tiempo aquí y ayer hizo sol casi todo el día. ¡Hasta mañana! [name]

118. Writing 4

1   **Model answer:** ¡Hola Álvaro!

Aquí en mi país tenemos tres opciones principales a los dieciséis años. Primero, puedes buscar un aprendizaje donde trabajas y recibes un sueldo. Es muy práctico y aprendes los conocimientos que necesitas. Es una opción con posibilidades.

Segundo, puedes seguir un curso de formación a tiempo parcial y, al mismo tiempo, hacer trabajo o voluntariado para ganar experiencia.

La tercera opción es continuar los estudios en el instituto. Esto es lo que me gustaría hacer en el futuro porque siempre he querido ser farmacéutico y necesito un título universitario. El mes pasado tuve la suerte de ayudar en una farmacia en mi pueblo y lo encontré fascinante porque es un trabajo muy responsable. Tienes que entender los efectos de las drogas y las medicinas. La gente a menudo pide consejo al farmacéutico.

Saludos [name]

Notes

Notes

Notes

Notes

Notes

Notes

Published by Pearson Education Limited, 80 Strand, London, WC2R 0RL.

www.pearsonschoolsandfecolleges.co.uk

Copies of official specifications for all Pearson qualifications may be found on the website: qualifications.pearson.com

Text, audio and illustrations © Pearson Education Limited 2017, 2021
Typeset and illustrated by Kamae Design, Oxford and Newgen Knowledgeworks
Produced by Cambridge Publishing Management Ltd and Newgen Publishing UK
Cover illustration by Kamae Design Ltd

The right of Vivien Halksworth to be identified as author of this work has been asserted by her in accordance with the Copyright, Designs and Patents Act 1988.

First published 2021

24
10 9 8

British Library Cataloguing in Publication Data
A catalogue record for this book is available from the British Library

ISBN 9781292412245

Copyright notice
All rights reserved. No part of this publication may be reproduced in any form or by any means (including photocopying or storing it in any medium by electronic means and whether or not transiently or incidentally to some other use of this publication) without the written permission of the copyright owner, except in accordance with the provisions of the Copyright, Designs and Patents Act 1988 or under the terms of a licence issued by the Copyright Licensing Agency, 5th Floor, Shackleton House, Hay's Galleria, 4 Battle Bridge Lane, London, SE1 2HX (www.cla.co.uk). Applications for the copyright owner's written permission should be addressed to the publisher.

Printed in Great Britain by Bell and Bain Ltd, Glasgow

Acknowledgements
Content written by Jacqui Lopez and Leanda Reeves is included.

Extract on page 22 from *Sara y las Goleadoras 6: El último gol*, © Laura Gallego García, Editorial Destino, 2010; Extract on page 46 from *El Club Dumas* by Arturo Pérez-Reverte, Alfaguara, 1993; Extract on page 54 from *Saber perder* by David Trueba, Editorial Anagrama, 2008; Extract on page 67 from *El Método Grönholm* by Jordi Galceran, Iberautor Promociones Culturales SL, 2003; Extract on page 76 from *Sara y las Goleadoras 5: Las Goleadoras no se rinden*, © Laura Gallego García, Editorial Destino, 2010; Extract on page 80 from Oxfam blog 'Las causas de la pobreza en el mundo', https://blog.oxfamintermon.org/las-causas-de-la-pobreza-en-el-mundo/ Accessed: 17 Aug 2021, FUNDACIÓN OXFAM INTERMÓN/OXFAM GB, 2021; Extract on page 113 from *Historia de una Maestra* by Josefina Aldecoa, Editorial Anagrama, 1990.

The author and publisher would like to thank the following individuals and organisations for permission to reproduce photographs:

123RF: Fizkes 17b; **Alamy Stock Photo:** Richard Wayman 9c, Tetra Images, LLC 60br, Image Source 69br, Gregg Vignal 110t; **Shutterstock:** Suhendri 2t, Andresr 4b, Terelyuk 6t, Goodluz 7t, Candace Hartley 8t, Shutterstock 11c, Peter Bernik 21c, Pressmaster 38br, KikoStock 44br, Maksim Shmeljov 50b, Shutterstock 57c, Erickson Stock 70b, Sorapop Udomsri 81br, Shutterstock 115tr.

Cover: Pearson Education Limited 2017

All other images © Pearson Education

Notes from the publisher
1. While the publishers have made every attempt to ensure that advice on the qualification and its assessment is accurate, the official specification and associated assessment guidance materials are the only authoritative source of information and should always be referred to for definitive guidance.

Pearson examiners have not contributed to any sections in this resource relevant to examination papers for which they have responsibility.

2. Pearson has robust editorial processes, including answer and fact checks, to ensure the accuracy of the content in this publication, and every effort is made to ensure this publication is free of errors. We are, however, only human, and occasionally errors do occur. Pearson is not liable for any misunderstandings that arise as a result of errors in this publication, but it is our priority to ensure that the content is accurate. If you spot an error, please do contact us at resourcescorrections@pearson.com so we can make sure it is corrected.